GRADES K–2

A Program for Creating a Healthy Learning Environment by Encouraging, Understanding and Respecting

No Putdowns is a program of
CONTACT Community Services, Inc., Syracuse, New York

Contributing Writers
Jim Wright, M.S., C.A.S.
Wendy Stein, M.A.
Stephanie Pelcher, M.S.

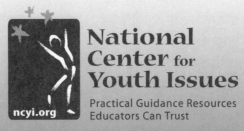

National Center for Youth Issues
Practical Guidance Resources
Educators Can Trust

ncyi.org

P.O. Box 22185 • Chattanooga, TN 37422-2185
423.899.5714 • 800.477.8277
fax: 423.899.4547 • www.ncyi.org

D1511944

Table of Contents

National Center for Youth Issues
Practical Guidance Resources
Educators Can Trust
ncyi.org

P.O. Box 22185 • Chattanooga, TN 37422-2185
423.899.5714 • 800.477.8277 • fax: 423.899.4547 • www.ncyi.org

ISBN: 1-931636-63-X (10-digit) 978-1-931636-63-6 (13-digit)

© 2006 National Center for Youth Issues, Chattanooga, TN
All rights reserved.

Revised 2006

Contributing Writers: Jim Wright, M.S., C.A.S.; Wendy Stein, M.A.; Stephanie Pelcher, M.S.
Cover Design and Page Layout: Phillip W. Rodgers
Published by National Center for Youth Issues
Printed in the United States of America

Why No Putdowns?

Schools and neighborhoods are becoming combat zones. So why worry about a few kids calling each other names?

"Why did you hit her?" "She looked at me wrong."

"Why did you pull that knife?" "He insulted me."

Children are dealing with serious issues of drug abuse, depression and peer pressure. So why bother with putdowns and a few hurt feelings?

A teenager feels the pain of rejection, being different, being alone. He drinks to fit it, so he won't be different, odd, or a loser.

An adolescent is overweight and can't face another year of name calling and taunts about his size. He hangs himself right before school resumes in September.

Why take time to deal with putdowns?

"I couldn't help it. He made me mad."

"It wasn't my fault. I just lost my temper."

"Once she makes me mad, there's nothing I can do about it."

"Nobody puts me down and gets away with it."

Violence has become any easy reaction to hurt feelings, and much of the violence starts with putdowns — a gesture, name calling, "disrespect." The putdowns grow louder and more abusive and the responses angrier and more reckless. And the violence to self and others spirals out of control — unless we teach our kids to STOP the spiral.

"Kids Today..."

"Kids today..." What adult generation hasn't started a lament about children with those words? It is practically a tradition to complain that "kids today" lack the values we grew up with.

"Our youth now love luxury; they have bad manners, contempt for authority, show disrespect for their elders, and love to chatter in place of exercise. They no longer rise when others enter the room. They contradict their parents, they chatter before company, they gobble their food and terrorize their teachers."

Socrates made those observations about children in the fifth century B.C., and we could dismiss out own "kids today" laments with the observation that every generation finds its next generation lacking. But we would be sticking our heads in the sand. Daniel Goleman writes in his book *Emotional Intelligence* that a massive survey of parents and teachers reveals that our children are more troubled emotionally than previous generations and that they are more lonely, depressed, angry, impulsive and aggressive.

Juvenile arrests for violent crimes have grown at an alarming rate. The news media are filled with accounts of violence in the schools and metal detectors installed at entrances. Alcohol and drug use are high among adolescents and teens. Teen pregnancy is on the rise. Reports of teen suicide have become all too common.

That is the dramatic and headline-grabbing news. But the distress is widespread, even among preschool and elementary school children. Parents and teachers report the increasing numbers of children are withdrawn, lacking in energy, unhappy or depressed. Many children act without thinking, don't pay attention or cannot concentrate. Aggressive behavior is disrupting home and school life as children argue, demand attention, interrupt, talk too much, tease critically, destroy property and anger easily.

We complain about children's lack of values and lack of discipline. But we are complaining about the society that we have created. We have all "gotten this way." Now what are we going to do about it? How can we start NOW to help our children become responsible, emotionally capable adults?

Goleman writes in *Emotional Intelligence* "At present we leave the emotional education of our children to chance, with ever more disastrous results. One solution is a new vision of what schools can do to educate the whole student, bringing together mind sand heart in the classroom."

The lessons are basic. If children hear a consistent message of respect and responsibility year after year, they can stop the spiral of violence. Putdowns among young children may seem relatively harmless. But those putdowns, the feelings that prompt them and the responses to them are the beginning of habits that will impact behavior for years to come.

Some educators question whether it is the job of the school to teach children interpersonal skills and emotional intelligence. However, character education expert Thomas Lickona writes, "Character education is as old as education itself. Down through history, education has had two great goals: to help people become smart and to help them become good."

It is not the job of the school alone. But schools can lead the way.

As on principal in a *No Putdowns* school told his staff, "Who is going to do it if we don't? Do we want the media to teach our children what it means to be a responsible adult?"

No Putdowns addresses issues integral to violence prevention, substance abuse prevention, conflict resolution and character education.

It focuses on building self-control, a sense of responsibility, self-worth, empathy, cooperation, respect and tolerance. It treats the school as a community and recognizes that members of that community have a right to a safe learning environment and a responsibility to create and preserve safety and trust for its members. The goal is to create an environment in which children feel safe to try new things, make mistakes, and learn, without fear of ridicule or recriminations.

No Putdowns involves parents and family and encourages children to take the message home. It brings parents to school for training and keeps them informed about the progress of the program. Nevertheless, even if some children do not learn these lessons at home, they can stop the spiral if they experience a school community that is caring, supportive and putdown-free.

Imagine declaring your school and its grounds a PUTDOWN-FREE ZONE. For many children, school is the one constant and safe place in their lives. Starting in kindergarten, they can experience school as a community of caring children and adults who treat one another with respect and resolve conflicts without verbal or physical violence. School becomes a model for how a community can be — people working together for the good of all.

These are idealistic goals for a ten-week elementary school program that teaches five simple skills: "Think About Why," "Stay Cool," "Shield Myself," "Choose a Response," and "Build Up." However, the ten-week program is only a beginning, a "starter tool kit" that you can use to build a safe school and a respectful community — and stop the spiral.

Section 1

Understanding *No Putdowns*

**A Program for Creating a Healthy
Learning Environment by Encouraging,
Understanding and Respecting**

What is *No Putdowns?*

No Putdowns is a comprehensive, school-based curriculum that can meet your needs for work in violence prevention, character development, substance abuse prevention skills, and life skill building. It was created as a school-wide program and experiences its greatest success when used that way. However, single grades or classrooms can also implement the program effectively.

Each *No Putdowns* book (K-2, 3-5 and 6-8) consists of a program guide for staff support and three grade level class activity guides. The formal program lasts approximately ten weeks, with two weeks devoted to each of the five skills. Each grade-level has fifty developmentally appropriate activities designed to extend, but not be dependent upon, activities of previous grade levels. Many teachers have found that the activities in the guides satisfactorily meet their needs. Others have adapted the lessons or made up some of their own. Each of these is an acceptable option. *No Putdowns* is designed to be part of your school day. Incorporate the lessons into your existing curriculum, or work the program into your day by using teachable moments rather than formal instruction time.

No Putdowns grew out of concern in Central New York with issues that are typical or problems facing other communities across the nation: culture intolerance, sliding academic performance, increasing violence in school and children's lack of respect. These issues were seen as major factors in youth suicide and substance abuse. Parents, educators and community members gathered to discuss how they could help children develop necessary emotional and life skills.

Given the scope of the problem, any program they proposed would have to be long term rather than a one-time workshop. It would be most effective if children could learn the necessary skills from adults whom they already trusted — school staff, with support and reinforcement from parents.

No Putdowns was developed under the auspices of CONTACT Community Services (a mental health agency providing educational services and telephone counseling) and the Onondaga County Department of Mental Health.

In 1991, the first version of the project was developed by twenty classroom teachers under the direction of professional staff developers and program director Margery Connor. It was piloted the following year within Onondaga County. It has since been revised based upon formal evaluation and field testing.

We are now seeing students who have "grown up" with *No Putdowns* at their schools. In those schools, the skills and language of *No Putdowns* are as common and natural as the ABCs.

Through the five skills of *No Putdowns*, students start looking at their own behavior and the behavior of others. The skills emphasize responsibility for one's own actions and choices, self-control, empathy, community building and effective listening and speaking skills.

The lessons are presented through a wide variety of formats, including dyad, small group and classroom discussion, writing, art and music, literature, independent projects, games and celebration, and media education. They are designed to meet the many styles through which students learn. Many lessons fit within existing social studies, language arts, physical education or fine arts curricula (and some will even lend themselves to math and science).

Through five skills, children become aware of their own power. They learn that power is the ability to manage one's feelings, to stop and think before responding rather than automatically lashing out. Power is the ability to make good choices, not the ability to hurt or control another. Students learn new powerful behaviors, such as helping others, apologizing when wrong, walking away from a fight, using constructive words instead of fists and putdowns, sharing, and including rather than excluding others.

It is not critical to have been involved with *No Putdowns* in early grades in order for it to be successful in later ones. However, it is helpful to be aware of the activities and concepts covered in other grades.

Outcomes

Upon completion of the ten-week instructional period, students (at an understanding appropriate to their grade) and staff will be able to:

- Recognize and understand the effects of putdowns on themselves and others
- Recognize that putdowns are used for a variety of reasons
- Develop strategies to reduce their own use of putdowns
- Recognize and use alternative communication skills
- Develop peaceful, non-abusive strategies to deal with putdowns and other conflict situations
- Demonstrate strategies for calming down
- List attributes, achievements, abilities of which they are proud
- Recognize that they have choices about how to respond in any situation
- Recognize and express appreciation, encouragement or compliments
- Demonstrate increased levels of respect in child-child, adult-child, and adult-adult interactions

Defining Putdowns

No Putdowns defines putdowns as negative or belittling words or actions that show disrespect toward a person or groups of persons. Putdowns are used both directly (to another person's face) and indirectly (to a third person about someone else.) They may be used because of fear, anger, ignorance, jealousy, need for power, frustration, lack of alternative communication skills, insecurity, habit, modeled behavior or humor. (Often, putdowns are disguised as humor — as seen in television sitcoms.)

Putdowns take many forms, both verbal and nonverbal:

- Dismissal or rejection, in the form of a critical or slighting remark
- Body language — rolled eyes, curled lip, shrugged shoulders, sneers
- Mimicking or mockery
- Words or actions used as weapons
- Self-putdowns
- Tone of voice, such as sarcasm or insincerity
- Stereotyping

Putdowns have a situational quality. Not only does a person's reaction depend upon the source of the putdown, it also depends upon circumstances. Putdowns hurt most when

- They are used in front of peers
- A loved one or someone you respect uses them
- They are used because of prejudice
- They are used repeatedly
- They hit a vulnerable area, something about which you are already insecure (family, appearance, abilities, body image)
- You are already sad, upset, frustrated or discouraged
- They lock you into a role or behavior ("You'll never be able to play soccer; you're a klutz.")

Skill 1: Think About Why

The key word for this first *No Putdowns* skill is AWARENESS. "Think About Why" invites children to begin to define, identify and investigate their use of putdowns. They begin to think about two essential questions:

- Why do I use putdowns?
- Why do other people use putdowns?

This skill urges children to stop and think before automatically responding to a putdown or other perceived threat with a putdown. Children discover that anger, hurt, fear, jealousy, ignorance and power are often underlying reasons for putdowns. By asking the other person for more information, active listening, and empathy, they can learn more about the motives behind a perceived insult. By taking the time to "think about why," a child may learn that a comment was actually intended as constructive criticism rather than a putdown. Or they sense that the putdown was motivated by strong emotions, and the best response is to show empathy rather than trade insults.

Issues of diversity and intolerance are explored in this skill and throughout the program because cultural, gender, ethnic, physical, lifestyle and other differences are very often at the root of putdowns and escalating conflict. Through more open communication, children discover they have more similarities than differences with the other person.

During these first two weeks of *No Putdowns*, children and adults become increasingly aware of the use and nature of putdowns. This growing awareness is the beginning of change. Although alternatives to putdowns are not fully explored in this skill, participants begin to think about their own responses and behavior.

continued on next page

Skill Development

Kindergarten

- Identification of feeling words
- Identification of strong feelings that provoke putdowns

Grade 1

- Vocabulary building
- Identification of feelings through nonverbal clues
- Identification of events or situations that cause strong feelings
- Practice identifying putdowns
- Discussion and practice of manners as expressions of respect

Grade 2

- Use of empathy in putdown situations
- Differentiation between putdowns and constructive criticism and discipline
- Exploration of chain of events that create a spiral of angry feelings and putdowns
- Exploration of relationship between feelings and actions
- Identification of putdowns on television

Grade 3

- Exploration of consequences of putdowns
- Discussion of television putdowns and humor
- Self-assessment of putdown use
- Further understanding of empathy as ability to put oneself in other person's shoes

Grade 4

- Development of feeling vocabulary through antonyms, pantomime, poetry and word games
- Self-assessment of putdown use
- Exploration of use of putdowns in advertising, especially use of stereotypes and name-calling

Grade 5

- Assessment of school climate through "scavenger hunt" for putdowns and encouragement
- Consideration of use and abuse of power
- Discussion of putdowns as an expression of power

Skill 2: Stay Cool

"Stay Cool" provides strategies for staying calm in stressful situations. "Take a moment, buy yourself some time," this skill teaches "Think before you respond; do not simply react." This second skill begins to raise the issues of self-control and choice. Children can choose to manage their feelings rather than allowing their feelings to control them. They learn specific strategies they can begin to use right away, recognize events and situations that are potential triggers for them personally, and identify consequences of losing their cool. This skill fits well into health studies or drug and alcohol prevention.

In older grades, this second skill continues to address issues of personal responsibility within a community as children consider people who stayed cool in the face of prejudice and other adversity in order to bring about positive change.

Skill Development

Kindergarten
- Introduction and practice of three specific strategies
- Count to ten
- Take deep breaths
- Say to yourself, "Freeze, please," or "Stay cool"
- Practice being still and peaceful
- Discussion of consequences of losing cool by considering behavior of favorite storybook characters

Grade 1
- Review of three basic strategies introduced in kindergarten
- Use of language and art for describing and understanding concept of staying cool
- Further discussion of consequences of losing cool by considering favorite fictional and historic characters

Grade 2
- Variations and practice of the three basic strategies
- Awareness of stress level through construction and use of "tension barometers"
- Use of role-plays for practice of techniques
- Choosing one strategy to practice for several days
- Identification of literacy characters who stayed cool

Grade 3
- Demonstration of an "eruption" of baking soda and vinegar as metaphor for losing cool
- Identification of personal physical signs of anger
- Use of muscle relaxation techniques to calm down
- Discussion of difference between staying cool and burying one's feelings

Grade 4
- Identification of personal stressors
- Identification of "stay cool" strategies that can interrupt cycle of stress
- Introduction of additional muscle relaxation exercises
- Exploration of importance of "keeping the situation in perspective" and the role of thought and language in how people view a situation or event
- Analysis of role of television on stress levels

Grade 5
- Review of strategies from earlier grades
- Identification of stressors and appropriateness and effectiveness of student's usual responses
- Emphasis on language skills in understanding concept of staying cool

continued on next page

Skill 3: Shield Myself

This skill teaches that children and adults can *shield* themselves from the devastating effects of putdowns. Their shield is a "force field" of confidence and self-worth. Children look at their own strengths and weaknesses, make honest assessments about themselves and recognize that they are worthy human beings. They do not have to do anything special to be special.

"Shield Myself" teaches that putdowns do not have to destroy one's sense of worth. Children investigate the harm they cause themselves through self-putdowns and negative self-talk, and they begin to substitute those self-denigrating habits with positive statements and affirmations. Older students also learn about goal-setting and planning as prerequisites to achievement. Although this lesson teaches that children do not have to be "stars" or excel to be worthy people, a sense of achievement enhances self-esteem and self-respect.

This third skill also looks at issues of diversity and celebration of individual differences and strengths.

Skill Development

Kindergarten
- Development of self-concept through creation of "All About Me" booklets
- Introduction to harm putdowns can cause to self-concept
- Introduction to shielding effect of confidence and positive self-talk

Grade 1
- Creation of personal shields
- Illustration and discussion of impact of positive self-talk and ability to achieve goals
- Identification of accomplishments
- Recognition that it is acceptable to make mistakes; mistakes do not have to destroy our confidence or ruin our day

Grade 2
- Identification of accomplishments or deeds of which students are proud
- Community building through sharing of interests and goals with class
- Discussion of what it means to be a good friend to oneself and others

Grade 3
- Emphasis on communication skills
- Focus on difference between bragging and speaking confidently
- Development of positive language skills by replacing "I can't" statements with more specific statements about limitations and abilities
- Introduction to positive responses to putdowns

Grade 4
- Development of positive self-talk
- Exploration of role of self-confidence and self-esteem as shields against putdowns
- Personal assessment of self-esteem by weighing likes and dislikes about oneself
- Learning to retain the constructive information in a comment and letting the putdown go

Grade 5

- Reflection on self-concept and how students think others see them
- Consideration of role of confidence in not only deflecting putdowns but preventing them
- Development of confidence through setting and reaching goals
- Importance of goal-setting and positive self-talk in achieving results

Skill 4: Choose a Response

When faced with a conflict, many children feel that they have few choices. They react by hitting, screaming, kicking, yelling — or withering in distress! "Choose a Response" stresses the role of choices in a child's life. Children (and adults) may not realize it, but they always have choices. However, some choices yield positive consequences and some, negative; children learn to consider those consequences before acting. After responding, they evaluate the results and decide whether the response would be effective the next time they are involved in a similar situation. Problem-solving models are provided for older grades to help children remember to consider alternatives and consequences.

This skill teaches nonviolent and constructive responses to putdowns and other conflicts. Often a child can respond with a clear and direct statement such as, "That feels like a putdown to me," or "That hurts my feelings."

In the first three grades, children learn about specific choices they can make and when they are most appropriately used. Older children begin to look at the importance of clear communication in resolving conflict and practice listening and speaking skills. By sixth grade, children learn to identify their own conflict resolution styles and recognize some predictable consequences of those styles.

Skill Development

Kindergarten

- Introduction of concept of choice
- Introduction of practice of three specific responses to conflict:
- Tell them to stop
- Walk away
- Tell an adult
- Identification of consequences of reacting rather than choosing a response

Grade 1

- Practice using the three specific responses (Tell them to stop, Walk away, and Tell an adult)
- Consideration of responses of fictional characters to conflict or putdowns
- Identification of responses of fictional characters to conflict or putdowns

Grade 2

- Practice using positive communication techniques of eye contact and listening
- Discussion and practice working together to reach agreement
- Consideration of safety issues in choosing a response
- Use of fable to identify responses and their consequences

continued on next page

Grade 3

- Practice using positive communication skills of listening, honesty, and consideration of other person's point of view

- Discussion of "letting it drop" as an appropriate response to a putdown or conflict

- Practice using problem-solving model STAR (Stop, Think, Act, Review)

Grade 4

- Practice using problem-solving model WHALE as reminder of choices (Words, Humor, Apologize, Let it drop)

- Demonstration of importance of "letting if go" if children choose to "let it drop"

Grade 5

- Practice using problem-solving model ACT (Alternatives, Consequences, Trial Run)

- Using of "I statements" in dealing with conflict

- Recognition of barriers to using *No Putdowns* responses

Skill 5: Build Up

"Build Up" is the opposite of put down, and the goal of this skill is to teach children to replace putdowns and encouraging and supportive communication and behavior. "Build Up" is also about building community, appreciating differences (and common traits), and pulling together as a class and a school to create a respectful, accepting and safe environment. Students learn about giving and receiving compliments, encouraging each other and working together. This skill, however, emphasizes sincere caring and respect, not empathy praise.

Skill Development

Kindergarten

- Practice giving verbal and nonverbal encouragement and compliments

- Discussion of differences and practice appreciating diversity

Grade 1

- Practice giving compliments and encouragement

- Identification of similarities and differences among classmates

- Recognition and appreciation of efforts of school members in creating an effective and nurturing community

Grade 2

- Practice giving and receiving compliments and encouragement

- Identification of "Build Up" behavior in media and in school

- Identification of ways to improve school community

- Practice with cooperative play

- Identification of person upon whom student can count for encouragement or help and recognition of responsibility of being available for others as well

Grade 3

- Practice giving and receiving compliments

- Recognition of contributions of others to school community

- Identification of build-ups in fiction and history

Grade 4

- Community building through encouragement and compliments
- Practice being a buddy by being a "secret buddy" to a classmate
- Practice working cooperatively on an art project
- Expression of written appreciation to community members who volunteer or help others through their jobs

Grade 5

- Focus on community building through cooperative work activities, common experiences and interests, and encouragement and compliments
- Consideration of effect of television on perception of differences

The *No Putdowns* video, performed by the Paul Robeson Performing Arts Company, Syracuse, New York, supplements the curriculum. It includes a five-minute *No Putdowns* rap song and short scenarios to illustrate the five skills.

Many schools have used the rap portion of the video in their kick-off events or as part of an assembly halfway through the program. The lyrics are included below in case some of your students would like to perform it. The rap song introduces the five skills and the *No Putdowns* chant.

The five skills scenarios have not been included in the lesson plans in the grade level books so that you can choose whether and when to show them. Teachers have used them to introduce a skill, as alternate lessons, or to wrap up a skill. Suggestions for discussion questions are provided below for your use. Adapt them as necessary for your grade level. Often, kindergarten and first grade teachers choose not to use the five scenarios since most feature older children and situations.

NO PUTDOWNS RAP

A woman stands at a podium speaking to a rally of parents, teachers, students and families.

"Welcome, everyone. We're here to talk about a problem that is sweeping the nation. It's in your homes, community and school. Everywhere you look, it's being done — makes who you are break and fall apart. Now that's a real work of art. You see, you have the power to stop it. What am I talking about? I'm talking about the infamous putdown."

They come and go, all through the day
From side to side and every which a way
Putdowns sometimes are not even said

But you know when you've been hit on the head
You dish it our — yeah
You take it in — yeah
That has to end
[Music begins]

Relaxing at home, minding your business
Watching a program of game show quizzes
Father walks in screaming and fussing
Why, what, when, it seems for nothing
He looks at you and all of a sudden
Does the one thing to push your button
You're feeling kinda hurt, trapped in a box
You'd do almost anything to take off the
   lock
Wait a minute, let me stand in his shoes
And ask a question or maybe two
Really listen to the bluesy blues
And understand why he did it to you
Really try to see deep inside
Guess you have to Think About Why

In class having a good time
Really involved and that's just fine
Somebody calls you a four-eyed egghead
The teacher yells out that shouldn't be said
But it's too late cause you already see red
Without thinking you dish it out instead
Tempers are flaring, it's this for that
But wait. Does it really have to be like that?
It's a bad program so you can change the
   station
Ignore, divert, distract the situation
And when you know that is where I'm
   coming from
In the end you don't feel dumb
At home, in school or on the block
Best strategy, Choose a Response!

No Putdowns, pass it around
Pass it around, *No Putdowns*
No Putdowns, pass it around
Pass it around, *No Putdowns*

Putdowns come in many forms and shapes
Most of the time there is no escape
Pouring down like rain on your face
Popping out from the least expected place
But you carry a big protective shield
It's kind of like a — force field
You have it every day, everywhere you walk
All you have to do is self-talk
I can be a good student
I can be a good friend
I can stay away from drugs
P.D.s can't get in
Shield your worth, shield your health
I'm the only person who can Shield Myself.

On the playground or in the neighborhood
Joking with friends that feels good
Then out of nowhere comes someone's
   aggression
You may feel anger, fear or depression
He's coming right at you to teach you a
   lesson
What do you do now — that's the question
All your emotions start to revolve
That won't help the problem get solved
Wait a minute, let me keep my cool
The wise man thinks, not the fool
I think I'll try the nonviolent way
Do my best to just walk away
Positive people use this rule
Talk it our, let it drop, Stay Cool!

Now in the community, home and school
There's one thing we all must do

Give love and respect in healthy rations
It's the right thing to do, always in fashion
Fills your heart with satisfaction
Replace putdowns with positive action

Spread it around universally
Goes hand in hand with diversity
Everyone has a right to respect
If someone denies you just put 'em in check
Compliment, helps others dream
You can inspire their self-esteem
Wish for the best and lots of good luck
Prepare for your future, Build Up.

No Putdowns, PASS IT AROUND
PASS IT AROUND, *No Putdowns*
No Putdowns, PASS IT AROUND
PASS IT AROUND, *No Putdowns*

No Putdowns, PASS IT AROUND
PASS IT AROUND, *No Putdowns*
Think about why…

No Putdowns, PASS IT AROUND
PASS IT AROUND, *No Putdowns*
Stay cool…

No Putdowns, PASS IT AROUND
PASS IT AROUND, *No Putdowns*
Shield myself…

No Putdowns, PASS IT AROUND
PASS IT AROUND, *No Putdowns*
Choose a response…

No Putdowns, PASS IT AROUND
PASS IT AROUND, *No Putdowns*
Build Up!

THINK ABOUT WHY

Time: 3 minutes

Scenario: On a busy morning, Dad is anxiously preparing for a job interview and trying to get his children ready for school. He is less than patient and the family is feeling the stress. The oldest daughter senses what is happening and explains the problem to her younger siblings. They all try to understand and cooperate to get everyone calmly out the door!

Introducing the scene:

- To avoid getting sidetracked by the composition of the family, explain that it is a group of actors and many not be characteristic of most families — the father is African-American, the older sister, Asian-American, and the younger siblings, white.

- Briefly describe the situation.

- Ask students to relate to the situation and think of an example from their own lives.

Discussion questions:

1. What is your house like in the morning?

2. What does the father do that is a putdown?

3. If someone is yelling at you, what do you do?

4. Did Danielle "think about why?" Did it work?

5. When have you been in a situation where you thought about why? Did it change your attitude or behavior?

6. Could you be as understanding as the kids in this video?

STAY COOL

Time: 2 minutes

Scenario: During a non-on-one basketball game, tension mounts and things start to get rough. The other children gather around the two boys and encourage them to fight. One player pushes the other, who trips on a baseball bat and falls. The other children laugh. As the boy picks himself up, he thinks about what he feels like doing to the others. He returns from his thoughts, looks at the group, picks up his baseball bat on the ground — and walks away.

Introducing the scene:

- Briefly describe the situation.

- Explain the difference between thinking about hitting or yelling and acting on those impulses.

- Note that the actors use language that is probably inappropriate for school ("Kick his butt").

Discussion questions:

1. Did the boy stay cool or was he a "wimp?" What, if anything, did he gain by his behavior? What, if anything, did he lose?

2. Why were the other children so eager for the two boys to fight?

3. Have you ever thought about doing something negative and then not acted on those thoughts? What stopped you? (Bring up the issue of consequences.)

4. What else could the boy have done and still stayed cool?

5. What do you think the coach/teacher should have done?

SHIELD MYSELF

Time: 3 minutes

Scenario: A group of drama students is complaining about a situation that happened in the school cafeteria. They start to put down the group that has been putting them down. Their teacher joins the discussion and talks to them about "self-talk."

Introducing the scene:

- Briefly describe the situation in the video.

- Define thespian.

- Note that the unhappy students are resorting to putdowns even though that is what has upset them!

- Ask students to listen for examples of self-talk.

Discussion questions:

1. Did the students feel better as they put down the "jocks"?

2. Can we control what others do or say to us?

3. Can we control our own thoughts, feelings and behavior?

4. Have you ever let something that someone did of said "get inside you"?

5. How do you keep the things that other people say and do from hurting you?

6. What self-talk phrases did you hear in the video? What self-talk phrases do you use?

7. If you have very different issues and tastes from most of the other kids, does that make you wrong?

CHOOSE A RESPONSE

Time: 2 minutes

Scenario: While the class is discussing a story, one boy is laughing and making rude comments. Sam responds to the teacher's question and is taunted by his classmates who call him names. The teacher urges, "No Putdowns" but the comments continue. Sarah tries to divert attention to other issues. Sam explains himself to the other.

Introducing the scene:

- Briefly set up the situation.

- Note that several different responses will be shown and students should watch for them. It especially illustrates ways not to respond!

Discussion questions:

1. What responses were used?

2. Are you ever afraid that others will make fun of you if you answer questions in class?

3. How can you respond if you are feeling angry, sad or afraid?

4. Is it ever acceptable to use physical violence as a response?

5. What could the teacher have done differently? (The teacher may be perceived as uninvolved and not in control of her class.)

6. Some of the people in the scene may be taken as stereotypical - the smart boy with glasses, the girls as peacemaker, the African-American boy as the troublemaker. Discuss the role of stereotypes in prompting putdowns.

BUILD UP

Time: 5 minutes

Scenario: Lisa is alone on stage trying to perform a song. She runs backstage and says she can't do it. Her friends offer encouragement and the teacher joins in with "You can do it" and other build up comments. Lisa goes on stage again with her friends and together they perform. Lisa soon gains confidence and the friends back away. As the song ends, the teacher and friends hug Lisa.

Introducing the scene:

• Briefly describe the situation.

• Explain that the friends' presence on stage is a physical show of support, but support does not have to be quite so dramatic!

Discussion questions:

1. How did Lisa's friends help her?

2. In what other ways might they have supported her?

3. Do you like people to encourage you?

4. What is the difference between encouragement and praise?

5. Should you be praised for everything you do?

6. How do you encourage friends and relatives?

7. How do you respond to a compliment? Do you give compliments?

Section 2

Using
No Putdowns

**A Program for Creating a Healthy
Learning Environment by Encouraging,
Understanding and Respecting**

Creating a Putdown-Free School

No Putdowns works best as a school-wide program with a goal of creating a putdown-free community. Creating that culture requires coordination and cooperation by all members of the school community. Buying into the creation of this PUTDOWN-FREE ZONE is important for all members of the school community. All students, all teachers, administrators, secretaries, counselors, bus drivers, cafeteria staff, everyone is part of the *No Putdowns* culture.

The adult members of the school community set the tone for *No Putdowns*. If they are enthusiastic and believe in it, children will become excited and take the messages to heart. If they give a halfhearted effort to it and are unwilling to look at their own communication habits, use of putdowns, or handling of conflict, the student population is going to sense that. They may wonder, "Why should we care?" Students are looking to the adults in their lives to model the *No Putdowns* behavior. School staff members are their role models, the key to the effectiveness of this program. School administrators report that the teachers who have the most success with the program are those who are enthusiastic and who "practice what they preach," by treating students and other adults with respect, listening, acknowledging children for their contributions, and valuing children and other adults.

Any adult who is in contact with students or their families can reinforce the skills. A powerful message is being sent to students as they notice that all staff members are speaking the same language and working within the same framework. If an argument is taking place in the cafeteria, the lunch aide or staff member on duty can use *No Putdowns* strategies and language to resolve it. Many principals display the *No Putdowns* poster in their offices and refer to the skills when disciplining students or ask students which skill they could have used to avoid the situation.

Many schools that have become involved with *No Putdowns* have devised their own projects, lessons and methods of extracurricular reinforcement.

The principal of Onondaga Road Elementary School, Syracuse, New York, makes it a point to teach a *No Putdowns* lesson to every class to demonstrate to staff and students his commitment to the program and its values.

Danforth Magnet School, Syracuse, used *No Putdowns* themes for its annual speaking contest.

Edgewater Elementary, Edgewater, Maryland, starts their school day with a *No Putdowns* message over their school TV system, after which the *No Putdowns* lessons are taught in the classrooms. Every adult in the building is assigned to a classroom to participate in the lessons!

Porter Elementary School, Syracuse, featured *No Putdowns* and its messages in the school newspaper, using the logo, slogans, and school news concerning the program.

Schools also make their own *No Putdowns* buttons, magnets, videos, and posters and have even silk-screened ties and t-shirts with program icons and themes.

No Putdowns is designed to be an integral part of school life, not "another thing to do." Be creative. When *No Putdowns* is incorporated into the language and culture of the school, it becomes a mindset, not just a ten-week program.

20 Ways to Create a No Putdowns Environment

1. Clearly define putdowns as any words or actions that are disrespectful of another person or group of persons and are used for reasons of anger, fear, power, humor, ignorance or learned behavior.

2. Make clear to everyone that putdowns are not tolerated. Draw attention to a putdown when you hear one.

3. Focus on build-up (supportive) behavior. Children and adults need daily practice replacing old putdowns with encouragers. Display build-up phrases on posters and banners. Incorporate the use of build ups rather than putdowns into all school functions - sports, assemblies, field trips, school publications.

4. Make daily No Putdowns announcements.

5. Provide clearly stated alternatives to putdowns.

6. Draw attention to the people who communicate without using putdowns.

7. Focus on positive rather than negative traits of people.

8. Decorate the school with posters, banners or art work that send the No Putdowns message.

9. When angry, deal with the situation without resorting to putdowns.

10. Avoid putdowns when reprimanding another person (child or adult).

11. Point out the positive consequences when putdowns are not used.

12. Point out the negative consequences when putdowns are used.

13. Be consistent, and model putdown-free communication. Children should not be using putdowns with other children or adults - and adults should not be using them with other adults or children.

14. Focus on differences among individuals as assets rather than problems.

15. Allow time for conflict resolution and anger management.

16. Take advantage of those "teachable moments" that occur in the classroom, hallway, cafeteria, playground or bus.

17. Encourage and support parental understanding and participation in reducing putdowns.

18. Recognize that there are many motivations for the use of putdowns: fear, jealousy, anger, power, inferiority or insecurity. Know that each individual is human and that change comes slowly, but that change can come. Hang in there.

19. Practice, practice, practice.

20. Model, model, model.

Teachable Moments throughout the School

Process daily happenings throughout your school within the framework of the five skills. Using the skills to deal with actual situations can help transform the lessons of *No Putdowns* from academic practice into daily living skills.

Use putdown or conflict situations as an opportunity to teach the skills or coach the participants as they use their new skills to resolve a problem. Step in if they need help. You can also freeze-frame a situation, briefly discuss what has happened so far, and consider consequences or various responses.

Be sure to point out situations that you observed in which the skills were used successfully. Congratulate students for working things out. Remind them to keep using the skills as effectively as they just did.

You cannot stop to process every incident, but you can deal with some of them and help your school environment become stronger. A teachable moment may be your *No Putdowns* lesson for the day!

The *No Putdowns* building coordinator is a vital link to the school wide implementation of the program. Often this role is filled by the building administrator, but any staff member (or even a small team) who is accessible and willing can take on the job. The building coordinator at one school noted that the most important job requirement "is to be the best cheerleader you can be. The building coordinator has to be enthusiastic and want to see the program succeed."

The building coordinator has several responsibilities, including advocating for the program and introducing it to three groups — staff, students and parents. (See Student Kick-Off and Taking It Home to Parents sections.)

Staff Involvement

No Putdowns is most successful when staff members are willing participants. It is very important for the school staff to have a voice in making the decisions about involvement. (A parent committee may also be involved in the decision.) Many schools take a vote or participate in a consensus-reaching exercise before making a final decision. Teachers and other school staff must be partners in this effort to transform children's attitudes and behavior. Bring the staff together for an introduction and discussion about participation in *No Putdowns*. Discuss what it will mean to become a *No Putdowns* school, and allow time for staff members to express their concerns or support. This can lead to a very honest discussion about the climate in the school and goals for improvement.

Before starting the program with students, arrange for staff development, either in a special workshop or as part of a faculty or grade level meeting. The training can be led by the building administrator or curriculum specialists.

The training familiarizes the staff with the concepts of *No Putdowns*. Rather than focusing on the activities, training time can be used to lay the groundwork for the school's involvement, plan school-wide activities and procedures and address any questions or concerns. The staff development time should establish the definition of putdowns as it will be used in the school and should ask the staff to analyze their own use of putdowns in professional and personal interactions. (See the initial training activity in the parent training section for an introductory exercise.) The staff training should be an opportunity for all faculty and staff members to come to a common understanding of what will be happening and assess how they can be most effective in their participation. The following chart was developed by the staff at Franklin Magnet School in Syracuse, New York, to help them define their expectations and goals.

Skill	What it looks like or means in our school
We Think About	Why We listen and follow adults' directions We respect all property
We Stay Cool	We use quiet voices We tell an adult if we have a problem
We Shield Ourselves	We feature our students in positive ways: Student of the week Plays and performances
We Choose a Response	We learn how to solve problems We choose peace
We Build Up	Our students and staff help us build our self esteem

During the formal ten-week program, include *No Putdowns* on the agenda for faculty or team meetings to discuss questions/concerns about the program as it evolves. Allow time for the teachers to discuss problems and successes and to brainstorm ideas. As a staff, you may decide to arrange additional events for students, staff or families, such as assemblies, displays, contests or guest speakers. (Even after the ten weeks, continue to include *No Putdowns* on meeting agendas, keep it in teachers' consciousness and relate it to special events and everyday practice.)

Remind teaching staff to complete the evaluation form that is printed at the end of each skill in the manuals. Ask them to monitor incidents of violence, either physical or verbal. Keep track of the numbers of visits to the health office, and observe how the class is behaving outside the classroom walls. These are all forms of evaluation (see Program Evaluation) and can help staff members plan for their future involvements in the program.

Scheduling

When implementing the program on a school-wide or grade-wide basis, it is important for all classrooms to begin and end each of the five skills at the same time. This will ensure that daily announcements and letters to families will be synchronized.

Select a ten-week time period with consideration given to holidays and vacation days, testing or other school events. Be sure that they entire school knows about the *No Putdowns* scheduling. The coordinator should send out a schedule to staff. Here is a sample:

To teachers and staff

We will be involved with *No Putdowns* for the next ten weeks.

Kick-off Assembly	Oct. 4
Skill 1	Oct. 7 - 18
Skill 2	Oct. 21 - Nov. 1
Skill 3	Nov. 4 - 15
Skill 4	Nov. 18 - 29 (Skill 4 is shortened by the Thanksgiving break. Wrap it up before the break.)
Skill 5	Dec. 2 - 13

Publicity

In many cities, *No Putdowns* schools have been featured in the news media because of the community's concern about reducing violence, abuse and addiction problems. No Putdowns attracts attention and interest because of its recognition that substantive changes in attitudes and behavior can impact school and community.

Coordinating Daily Announcements

No Putdowns schools start each day with a skill-related announcement over the loud speaker. Ten announcements for each skill are provided in this manual. (see Daily Announcement). School staff or students may read these or school-generated announcements.

The building coordinator also distributes supplies (posters, pins, pencils, banners) and orders additional supplies and monitors progress through teacher evaluations. (See Program Evaluation.)

Student Kick-off Event

Get your school off to a running start with a school-wide launch of *No Putdowns*. Make the start of the program an event, a rally, an opportunity to generate some enthusiasm and create community feeling. Hold a special gathering or tie the kick-off event into existing school spirit assemblies or weekly programs. Most importantly — MAKE IT FUN!

Use your imagination, and create your own program. Or try some of these ideas that other *No Putdowns* schools have used:

- Invite guest speakers — local sports figures, coaches or performers, to talk to the school. With a little preparation, these guests speakers can address the issues of *No Putdowns*: respect, trust, keeping a cool head, thinking before responding, building teamwork, self-esteem.

- Choose readings and music related to *No Putdowns* themes. Present skits related to the five skills.

- Tie the launch of the program into the launch of an important or well-known community event, such as the start of a sports season, community food drive, or a race to raise money for an organization.

- Invite older students to talk to younger students about issues related to *No Putdowns*.

- Organize a school-wide community service project, such as planting trees or flowers or cleaning up a playground. Help children understand that *No Putdowns* is about making their community more friendly, peaceful and cooperative, and that they must all do their part.

- Invite local entertainers (singers, magicians, actors) to perform relevant materials.

- Begin a countdown to *No Putdowns* a week or two before the kick-off event to build anticipation and curiosity.

- Your community may have a performer who specializes in shows for school children and whose materials tie into many of the *No Putdowns* themes.

Making parents aware of the program is an important step in creating a putdown-free environment. Get the parents involved! Let them know what the program is about and how they can reinforce the five skills with their children. Look for any opportunity to bring them into the process — through homework, letters introducing each skill (see samples at the end of this section), and parent training within the first three weeks of the launch of the program in the school. The building coordinator or another staff person can conduct this training, or a *No Putdowns* representative may be available.

Parent Training

Schedule a one-and-one-half to two hour parent training session as close to the student kick-off event as possible. Student enthusiasm generates parental interest. Scheduling the training as a special event rather than part of the regular parent teacher association business meeting is likely to attract more participants.

Parents will want to know why the school is using the program and what positive results they can expect to see.

- As an opener, ask parents to break into groups and discuss these three questions:
  - ➤ What are putdowns?
  - ➤ Why do people use putdowns?
  - ➤ When do they hurt the most?

By helping parents increase their awareness of putdowns in their own lives and in the world at large (government, athletics, media), they are better able to support the program at home.

- Point out a few mind-boggling statistics:
  - ➤ By the time a child is 15 years old, he or she has heard 100,000 putdowns.
  - ➤ About 77% of what individuals hear each day is negative.
  - ➤ If you send a positive message, there is a 90% chance you will receive a positive message in return,
  - ➤ A child's mind is like a computer. Information is constantly being fed into it, and for every negative idea put in, a child needs twelve positive comments to balance it.
  - ➤ About 92% of adults fired from corporate jobs are fired for problems with their interpersonal skills.

- Explain each of the five skills, and provide handouts and copies of the small posters to hang in their homes as reminders to their children. List specific ways parents and families can reinforce the five skills. (A handout is provided in the letters section.) Explain that the school will spend two weeks on each skill and parents will receive a letter as each new skill is introduced.

- Ask for volunteers to comment on common family situations in which putdowns are often used! Ask parents to quickly respond as they normally would if a child:
  - ➤ just dropped his or her book bag at the door
  - ➤ had a messy room
  - ➤ was fighting with a sibling
  - ➤ did poorly on a test

They may be surprised to see how easily putdowns roll out of their mouths! Practice alternative responses.

- Allow plenty of time for discussion. Parents usually have many questions about *No Putdowns*, children's behavior, and family communication. Break into groups, and then have the groups report their questions and concerns. Or ask for questions on index cards and use them as springboards for discussion. Encourage parents to offer ideas to one another. The facilitator does not have to be the expert.

Letters and Handouts Concerning No Putdowns

Following are examples of handouts for training and letters that you can send home with children to inform parents and family about the *No Putdowns* project. Revise as necessary to meet your school's needs. Letters should be sent to families of all children in the program. Determine who in your school has responsibility for home letters (administrator, building coordinator, individual teachers).

Introducing No Putdowns

Dear Parents,

Today our school started a new and exciting project called *No Putdowns*. We believe it will have an impact on our school community and in your home. The goal of this ten-week project is to teach children to recognize and understand the effects of putdowns. Children will develop strategies for reducing their own use of putdowns and responding to others' putdowns without violence.

We will spend two weeks on each of these five skills:

"Think About Why," "Stay Cool," "Shield Myself," "Choose a Response," and "Build Up."

The first skill we will focus on, "Think About Why," helps children learn to identify putdowns and think about why they or others might have used them. What feelings or situations prompt putdowns?

We appreciate your support and reinforcement of the skills taught in this very important project.

Please call if you have any questions.

Sincerely,

Introducing "Stay Cool"

Dear Parents,

We want to keep you updated on our progress with *No Putdowns*. For the past two weeks, we have been working on "Think About Why." Students have been learning to identify and define putdowns and understand why putdowns are used.

Today we introduced the second skill in our program, "Stay Cool." Students will learn some specific anger management strategies, such as taking a deep breath, counting to ten or relaxing the muscles. Through these techniques, they learn to "buy some time" before responding. Children will look at their own behaviors and that of others to analyze what they do when angry and what they could do differently.

As always, please don't hesitate to call if you have any questions or comments about *No Putdowns*.

Sincerely,

Introducing "Shield Myself"

Dear Parents,

We have completed our work on "Stay Cool" and have seen our students taking steps to recognize and manage their anger.

Today we move on the "Shield Myself," where children will work on ways to protect themselves from putdowns by recognizing and preserving self-esteem. They will focus on what makes them special and unique. However, they will also look at the difference between bragging and being confident. This is not about hollow claims or egotism. It is about a simple appreciation and respect for oneself. With a strong sense of self, children are better able to deal with putdowns and prevent those negative comments and behaviors from devastating them.

We hope that your child is haring *No Putdowns* lessons with you and is enthusiastic about participating in the program.

Sincerely,

Introducing "Choose a Response"

Dear Parents,

Our work with *No Putdowns* continues. We have completed three skills: "Think About Why," "Stay Cool" and "Shield Myself." Today we introduced "Choose a Response," in which children begin to recognize and assess their choices in a conflict situation. Some of the choices they will consider include:

Asking the other person to stop
Walking away
Telling an adult
Letting it drop
Using humor

We hope you are hearing about these skills from your child and are helping him or her use them at home.

We appreciate your continued support.

Sincerely,

Introducing "Build Up"

Dear Parents,

Today we introduced the final *No Putdowns* skill, "Build Up." Students will learn to give and receive build ups in place of putdowns. Build ups are encouragement, compliments and common courtesies. In a school where build ups replace putdowns, we will have a stronger, more positive and supportive community.

As we all know, we often need a word of encouragement to keep us going! Productivity and morale will improve when there is recognition of effort and achievement. However, we are not encouraging empty praise!

Although our formal *No Putdowns* program will end with this skill, the concepts will continue to be reinforced. Thank you for your support. We hope this has been a fun and worthwhile program for your child.

Sincerely,

 **Think About Why**

 **Stay Cool**

 **Shield Myself**

 **Choose a Response**

 **Build Up**

...pass it around!

What Is
No Putdowns
All About?

- It recognizes the effects of putdowns.
- It rejects the use of putdowns.
- It replaces putdowns with build ups.
- It offers alternatives.
- It teaches respect.

How can family members reinforce; the work of *No Putdowns*?

1. Use the language of the program — Think About Why, Stay Cool, Shield Myself, Choose a Response, Build Up.

2. Refer to the skills in daily interactions.

3. Observe the use of putdowns at stores, restaurants, on television and radio.

4. Think about establishing an incentive program to reinforce use of the skills.

5. Tune into your own use of putdowns.

6. Emphasize positive communication: Listening, eye contact, questions, paying attention to the speaker, fighting fair, and encouraging rather than discouraging. These are skills that can be practiced and used.

7. Remind your children that as parents and as adults, you have a right and responsibility to correct their behavior and that there is a difference between constructive criticism and reprimands — and putdowns. However, when you need to get a point across, try to do it without a putdown. Instead of "You're so sloppy or lazy." Try "After you pick up your toys, you can go play." You can get your point across without a putdown.

These ten-second announcements reinforce each of the five skills. Choose a student to read an announcement each day over the loudspeaker or in class. Use the announcements as springboards for discussion.

Daily announcements related to the *No Putdowns* themes are a way to keep the program going even after the ten weeks of the formal program have ended. Encourage students to write new daily announcements.

Skill 1: Think About Why

1

No Putdowns is just beginning
Let's take a look at what it's bringing
Time to think, time to choose
Time to put yourself in the other person's shoes.
Think About Why you put down,
and remember —
No Putdowns — Pass it around!

2

So you think you're just fooling around
But stop and ask, "Why put people downs?"
No Putdowns — Pass it around!

3

How do you feel today?
Happy? Sad? Angry? Scared?
Tune into your feelings.
Tune out to putdowns.
No Putdowns, Pass it around!

4

Hurting others hurts you in the long run —
think about it.
No Putdowns, Pass it around!

5

Think before you act, it can make a difference.
Here's an example, just a for instance:
When you get put down,
Try something new —
Don't put down because they put down you.
No Putdowns, Pass it around!

6

Break the habit of putdowns.
Think about what you're saying
before you say it.
No Putdowns, Pass it around!

7

That person you put down has feelings too.
No Putdowns, Pass it around!

8

Maybe you feel mad
Maybe you feel blue
Maybe something is upsetting you
But don't take it out on your friends,
Think about the message you send.
No Putdowns, Pass it around!

9

When we putdown
We hurt another person's feelings.
Let's think before we speak.
No Putdowns, Pass it around!

10

It someone puts you down,
You may want to ask,
"Why did you say that to me?
What did you mean?"

Maybe the comment wasn't what it seemed.
No Putdowns, Pass it around!

Skill 2: Stay Cool

1

You've been thinking about why.
Now let's learn about STAY COOL
All the ways to cool off,
Without jumping in a pool.
No Putdowns, Pass it around!

2

The weather forecast for school
today is STAY COOL.
No Putdowns, Pass it around!

3

Feeling upset? Stay Cool.
Take a deep breath — that's one tool.
No Putdowns, Pass it around!

4

If a putdown makes you start to get hot,
count to ten,
Cool down again.
Stay Cool — that's the rule.
No Putdowns, Pass it around!

5

Don't answer a putdown with a putdown,
Think twice, keep it on ice!
Take a deep breath — like this — (inhale)
Stay Cool,
No Putdowns, Pass it around!

6

Don't be too quick to react,
Don't be so fast to jump to conclusions
Just take a second, relax, stay cool
Keep the peace here in your school.
No Putdowns, Pass it around!

7

Someone just put you down,
So now a putdown is on the tip of your tongue.
Stop! Stay Cool!
No Putdowns, Pass it around!
Pass it around! *No Putdowns*!

8

It's okay to be angry, but don't take it out on
someone else. Stay Cool.
No Putdowns, Pass it around!

9

Act and react in positive ways
It works wonders
And smoothes out your days.
Stay cool
No Putdowns, Pass it around!

10

When your temperature starts climbing
and you feel like exploding,
Take a moment to relax, keep calm, stay cool.
No Putdowns, Pass it around!

Skill 3: Shield Myself

1

I don't need to take putdowns to heart.
Shield Myself — that's a good start.
No Putdowns, Pass it around!

2

Remember — think positive
Remember — Think SHIELD MYSELF
No Putdowns, Pass it around!

3

We can't be a star at everything we do.
Some people shine at spelling,
some people shine at art,
Nobody shines at everything,
And remembering that would be smart.
No Putdowns, Pass it around!

4

Feeling good about what you say or do
Makes the day go better for you.
No Putdowns, Pass it around!

5

When you look in a mirror, you see YOU
The only one of your kind!
You can build an invisible force field
That shields you against putdowns.
No Putdowns, Pass it around!

6

Shield Myself means feeling good about me
I don't have to brag, and I don't have to lie.
No Putdowns, Pass it around!

7

When you put me down, I can take it
I have self-esteem, and I don't fake it.
When you put me down, I can take it,
I have confidence, and you can't break it.
No Putdowns, Pass it around!

8

Respect yourself
Respect each other
No Putdowns, Pass it around!

9

I Shield Myself, and that means
I don't let putdowns destroy me.
I shield myself and that means
I don't have to put
you down to make me feel good!
No Putdowns, Pass it around!

10

Shield yourself means knowing
your strengths and flaws
And feeling good about who you are.
No Putdowns, Pass it around!

Skill 4: Choose a Response

1

It's not always easy to know what to do.
But we always have choices — really it's true!
No Putdowns, Pass it around!

2

Walk away? Talk it out?
Ignore the problem?
You decide what's best.
No Putdowns, Pass it around!

3

When someone tries to put you down,
think about
why they're doing it, stay cool,
and decide what's
the best thing you can do —
for you and the other person
No Putdowns, Pass it around!

4

When a putdown comes down on you,
are you learning what to do?
Stop is a word that you can say,
Or you might choose to walk away.
No Putdowns, Pass it around!

5

Tell putdowners to stop,
and you know what — they may.
Or pretend you don't hear it and walk away.
Or tell an adult, that too is okay,
whatever you choose cam make your day.
No Putdowns, Pass it around!

6

You're studying skill four
You're making decisions
You're learning how to avoid collisions.
No Putdowns, Pass it around!
Pass it around, *No Putdowns*.

7

It's up to you. You have the power to make good
choices, choices that keep a putdown
situation from getting worse.
No Putdowns, Pass it around!

8

Guess what? You don't have to respond.
You can let it drop without a sound.
No Putdowns, Pass it around!

9

If you get put down it's okay to tell an adult that
someone is trying to give you a hard time.
Sometimes a parent, an older brother or sister,
teacher, coach, of counselor can help —
without causing more problems for you.
No Putdowns, Pass it around!

10

Before you respond, look at your choices,
It's not always about raising your voices.
Choose the response that passes the test,
The one that makes things turn out the best.
No Putdowns, Pass it around!
Pass it around, *No Putdowns*.

Skill 5: Build Up

1

BUILD UP is the opposite of putdown.
See if you can take the idea out to your town.
Build up, don't put down,
With build ups, you make a happy sound.
No Putdowns, Pass it around!

2

United we stand, divided we fall
That's why build ups are good for us all.
No Putdowns, Pass it around!
Pass it around, *No Putdowns*.

3

Build ups don't have to be gushy,
Build ups don't have to be mushy,
Build up by showing some courtesies
Just by saying thank you or please.
No Putdowns, Pass it around!

4

We all need some support
and encouragement sometimes.
Be a friend to someone who needs a kind word.
No Putdowns, Pass it around!

5

Build ups make the school a better place to be.
When you are kind to others, it is contagious.
Kindness catches on.
No Putdowns, Pass it around!
Pass it around, *No Putdowns*.

6

If you like receiving compliments,
wait until you try giving them!
It feels really great.
No Putdowns, Pass it around!

7

Today is I Appreciate You Day!
Let the people in your life
know that you value them!
No Putdowns, Pass it around!

8

It is up to each one of us to make
the school community a supportive
and positive place.
We can do that by treating
each other with respect.
Respect is a build up!
No Putdowns, Pass it around!

9

When you build up others,
you build up yourself too.
No Putdowns, Pass it around!
Pass it around, *No Putdowns*.

10

Build up, don't put down,
Preserve that *No Putdowns* spirit
all year round.
No Putdowns, Pass it around!

Pass it around, *No Putdowns*.

Some common questions and concerns come up in *No Putdowns* schools.

"I don't have time to teach another program."

Time is always an issue for busy educators. When teachers are asked to present a new program, many sigh, "How can I fit one more thing into the day? Don't ask me to do any more!"

No Putdowns recognizes the time constraints of the teacher. It is not meant to be a major interruption to the school day. Although lessons range from 10 to 30 minutes each, many can be presented within the context of a regular subject area — reading and writing, social studies, music, art, physical education, even math! On some days, you might even choose to skip the *No Putdowns* lesson if an appropriate "teachable moment" arises (for example, a putdown situation in the classroom, a student's losing his or her cool, a build-up or community-building opportunity.) You can turn the everyday events of the classroom, or the everyday topics you cover into opportunities to reinforce and model *No Putdowns* skills.

Schools using the program for several years report that consistent use of *No Putdowns* language and modeling of the skills are more relevant to success than the actual amount of time devoted to formal lessons. However, they also report that the time spent on skill building has saved them time in the long run — time formerly spent on classroom management.

"The putdowns have increased since we started using *No Putdowns*!"

Don't worry, that is typical. Over the years, teachers have reported that putdowns seem to escalate at the beginning of the program. Focusing on a particular behavior often intensifies the behavior for a short time. But it will pass, and then you will see putdowns start to decrease.

"Are we making any progress?"

You take one step forward, you take two back. At least that's how it feels sometimes. You may not see significant changes right away, but once you begin pointing out putdowns, a child can't help but notice his or her own use of them, become more aware of them, and THINK about what he or she is saying. Don't give up. Awareness has taken root! Keep the message out there. The success of the program depends on repetition of the message — in the classroom, on the playground, at home. Research has shown it takes at least six weeks to incorporate behavioral changes, so don't give up. Learning these skills is a lifelong process, but you are planting the seeds, you are increasing children's awareness. If you are using this on a school wide basis, positive peer pressure will also bring results, as children start to call each other on their putdown behavior.

"I feel as if we are repeating lessons from other programs."

No Putdowns does present some of the same concepts as other character education, violence prevention, life skills, and drug prevention programs. *No Putdowns* addresses anger management, stress management, conflict resolution, communication and community building, as well as issues of peer pressure, alternatives to violence, tolerance, self-discipline, and healthy life choices.

If children complain, "We've already done this," acknowledge it, and make the connections between what *No Putdowns* and the other programs are about. (The bottom line on that is self-respect and respect for others!)

"My students complain that they already did *No Putdowns* last year."

Ideally, *No Putdowns* is a school wide program with three books ranging from kindergarten all the way up to eighth grade!

They will "grow up" with *No Putdowns*. Although there may seem to be some repetition, the program progresses in sophistication of concepts and strategies. Ask children to be patient, even if an activity seems familiar to them. Ask them to go along with it and to be willing to see that it is taking them to a new place. A principal in one Syracuse school pointed out that the repetition of the same message from a different teacher each year is a great strength of the program.

As a student moves through the grades with *No Putdowns*, there should be a cumulative effect felt in skill building. For that reason, it may be very helpful to have older students interact with younger students on the skills. Sometimes children will listen to other children better than they do adults, and older students will feel good about themselves as they are given positions of importance. They will often act in more

appropriate ways as they feel that they are role models. Younger students will learn from others and feel connections with "the big kids" instead of holding them in fear or awe. Peer work keeps the program alive for the students who have been in it for awhile. At the same time, it provides incentive for the younger students to stay involved.

"Our materials and copying budgets are limited!"

Each lesson lists the necessary materials for that day; however, most materials are readily available in any school. No expensive equipment or supplies are required. If your copying budget is limited, many of the lessons that require worksheets can also be done on note paper or in journals if you provide a model of the page for the class. If you do not have the suggested book(s) for a lesson, ask the librarian for other suggestions. In some cases, an alternative activity that does not require any books is provided within the lesson plan.

Monitoring the progress and assessing the outcomes in your school are essential steps that allow you to make adjustments where necessary and demonstrate program effectiveness. Several evaluation strategies are suggested below, along with sample forms for each. In addition, a skill evaluation is included at the end of each skill in the program guides; these can be compiled and used for formal evaluations as well.

Anecdotal reports. Watch and note attitude and behavioral changes. Are students using the vocabulary of the program? Are they observing behaviors in themselves and others? Are they moving beyond observation and making changes?

Discipline referrals. Monitor the number of discipline referrals for the school.

Student surveys. Ask students for their perceptions of changes in the classroom or school. Older students can use the included form. Use interviews or small group discussion with kindergarten and first grade students.

Self-assessment. Ask staff and students to record their perceptions of their own progress in reducing use of putdowns. In some grades, this strategy is used within lessons.

Staff-assessments. Ask staff for feedback part way through the program and following the completion of the ten weeks.

Pre- and Post-tests. Have students take the same test at the beginning and end of the ten week period, and compare results. For kindergarten and first grade children, this may be done orally or in a group discussion, keeping track of responses.

Anecdotal Report

Date/Time:

Location:

Description of event:

No *Putdown Skills* **Used/Observed:**

Outcome:

Date/Time:

Location:

Description of event:

No *Putdown Skills* **Used/Observed:**

Outcome:

Date/Time:

Location:

Description of event:

No *Putdown Skills* **Used/Observed:**

Outcome:

Date/Time:

Location:

Description of event:

No *Putdown Skills* **Used/Observed:**

Outcome:

Discipline Referral Report

Week of _____

Number of interruptions in class time due to:

_____ Talking

_____ Physical contact (poking, pushing, etc.)

_____ Talking

_____ Physical contact (poking, pushing, etc.)

_____ Fighting

_____ Annoyances (slamming books, paper airplanes, note-passing)

_____ Name Calling

_____ Need for adult intervention

Number of discipline-related referrals to:

_____ School office

_____ Health office

_____ Other (detention, etc.)

Number for conversation/communication regarding discipline issues with:

_____ Parents

_____ Bus driver

_____ Cafeteria staff

_____ School administration

_____ Special services

Notes/comments:

Student Survey

You have been working with *No Putdowns* for ten weeks. Please answer the following questions as truthfully as possible.

1. Do you use the *No Putdowns* skills? _____ Yes _____ No

2. Do you see other students using the skills? _____ Yes _____ No

3. Have the skills affected you in any way? Explain.

4. Do you think there have been any changes in how people in your school treat each other since *No Putdowns* started? Explain.

5. What is the most important lesson you have learned from *No Putdowns*?

Staff Assessment

Teacher Name _____

Grade _____

1. What skill are you currently working on?

2. How are you using the materials? Are you using the activities provided in the books, making up your own, or both?

3. Please describe other activities you have used.

4. Please comment on the appropriateness of the activities for your grade level.

5. Have the skills transferred to daily life? Are you seeing any positive behavioral changes? Please provide examples.

6. Have you encountered any problems or do you have any concerns, suggestions, etc?

Student Pre- and Post- Test

1. Describe or define putdown.

2. How often do you use putdowns?

    ☐ Never   ☐ Rarely   ☐ Often   ☐ Always

3. Whom do you put down most?

4. How do you calm down when you are angry?

5. What do you do when someone puts you down?

6. Do you think your classmates are supportive and encouraging?

7. What do you think sets off most of the fights in your school?

Keeping It Going

Old habits die hard, especially bad habits! Breaking the putdowns habit requires more than ten weeks. Keep the message out there after the ten weeks are completed. Continue to reinforce the message throughout the school year at all school events. *No Putdowns* may have been competed, but you are a *No Putdowns* school year round. To keep it going:

- Run mini-sessions for new students who missed the project. Experienced students could assist with the lessons.

- Have a school-wide assembly or *No Putdowns* theme day.

- Run mini-sessions for new teachers and staff.

- Create a link between *No Putdowns* skills and other school activities, such as school concerts, plays, newspaper, or new units of study.

- Keep talking about putdowns, keep pointing them out, and keep using *No Putdowns* language.

- Hold art contests or exhibits that display *No Putdowns* art. Students can create posters, banners, T-shirts, aprons, ties, and so on.

- Talk to parents about putdowns when you meet with them. Ask for feedback on children's use of the skills at home.

- Keep it in children's consciousness during summer vacation too. Emphasize "Stay Cool" as a great theme for summer activities. Have students draw posters relating the skills to summer fun or role play the skills in camp, sports, or family vacation situations.

JUST KEEP DOING IT as a way of school life. It will become part of the school culture.

GRADE
K

**A Program for Creating a Healthy
Learning Environment by Encouraging,
Understanding and Respecting**

Kindergarten

	NO PUTDOWNS SKILLS				
SOCIAL COMPETENCIES	**Skill 1:** Think About Why	**Skill 2:** Stay Cool	**Skill 3:** Shield Myself	**Skill 4:** Choose a Response	**Skill 5:** Build Up
Communication Skills	X	X		X	X
Empathy	X			X	X
Self-worth			X	X	X
Respect	X	X	X	X	X
Self-control		X		X	
Community Building					X
Conflict Resolution				X	
Anger/Stress Management	X	X	X	X	X
Problem-solving				X	X
Violence Prevention		X		X	X

KINDERGARTEN ACTIVITIES

Skill 1: Think About Why

Skill 2: Stay Cool

Skill 3: Shield Myself

Skill 4: Choose a Response

Skill 5: Build Up

GRADE
K

SKILL 1

Think About Why

A Program for Creating a Healthy Learning Environment by Encouraging, Understanding and Respecting

Introduction to *No Putdowns*

Putdowns are words or actions that are disrespectful to another person, place, or thing. They are used for reasons of power, anger, fear, jealousy, habit, humor, frustration, or modeled behavior. See the teacher's manual for a full discussion of putdowns.

 Time Needed: 15 minutes

 Purpose: Students will be introduced to *No Putdowns* and Skill 1 "Think About Why."

 Main Ideas: Entire school is participating in this program. Putdowns are words or actions that are disrespectful. Putdowns are often caused by strong feelings.

Materials: None

Using This Activity

1. Bring the class together for a discussion.

2. Ask your class, "Has anyone ever hurt your feelings or said or done something that made you feel terrible?" [Students may talk about name-calling, pushing, spanking, scolding, being yelled at, being teased, and so on.]

3. After they have responded, refer to the incidents dealing with name-calling, being ignored or excluded, teasing, and similar actions. Tell the class, "When someone makes fun of us, we call that a putdown."

4. Explain that "The entire school is starting a ten-week project called *No Putdowns*. The goals for the school and the class are to not use putdowns and to learn how to respond if someone does put you down.

5. Tell the class, "We're going to be learning five skills in the next ten weeks. The first one is called 'Think About Why.' This week and next week, we're going to do activities that help us identify putdowns and try to figure out the feelings that lead to putdowns."

If the school is involved in other character education efforts, this is a good time to make the connection so that students see that *No Putdowns* is another piece of the puzzle of how to treat themselves and others.

6. Wrap up this introduction by asking, "Do you have any idea why you say mean things to your brothers, sisters or classmates? [Children may answer that someone made them mad, they couldn't do something they wanted to do, or the other person had something they wanted.] Point out that they had strong feelings when they used the putdown, and strong feelings can be confusing.

Feeling Words

 Time Needed: 15 minutes

 Purpose: Students will learn feeling words.

 Main Idea: Feelings are normal and natural. What we do with them when we experience them is important.

 **Materials:** Chart paper and marker

Using This Activity

1. Ask the class for a list of feeling words. To prompt answers, you might ask about particular situations: How do you feel on your birthday? How do you feel when you are home alone? Write the feeling on the paper. [At this age, the list may be short: happy, sad, mad, glad, scared, excited.] Post the list in a prominent place.

2. Explain that all those feelings are acceptable. "It is okay to feel mad or scared, even though those feelings may be confusing or make you feel sick! We have to learn to deal with our feelings, especially the ones that sometimes get us into trouble, such as anger, jealousy or frustration. It is not the feeling that is wrong. It is what we do with it when we feel that way." You may want to give some examples at this point.

3. Wrap up this short session by promising that *No Putdowns* will help them learn to recognize and deal with their feelings.

Invite children to bring in new feeling words, or you may want to teach them some other feeling words. Add the new words to the list on the chart. The list of feelings can be used for reading readiness.

Although this activity does not specifically look at putdowns, ask students to listen and watch for putdowns so they can tell the class about them tomorrow.

At the beginning of each *No Putdowns* session, ask two or three students if they have used or heard any putdowns, and invite them to tell the class about them. Caution them not to use the names of other people involved. If no one responds, congratulate them for a job well done. If any students did use putdowns, ask them what they were feeling when they used them.

A reproducible sheet for Happy/Sad cutouts is included at the end of this activity.

You could also add some situations that have actually happened in class without referring to particular children.

Happy/Sad Stick Puppets

 Time Needed: 20-30 minutes each activity

 Purpose: Students will be able to differentiate between happy and sad feelings.

 **Main Idea:** Different circumstances evoke feelings of happiness and sadness.

 **Materials:** Copies of Happy/Sad faces, scissors, tongue depressors or Popsicle sticks, stapler

Using This Activity

Activity 3

1. Have each student make a happy/sad stick puppet by cutting out a happy face and a sad face and attaching them back-to-back to the stick.

2. Ask each student to print his/her name on the stick part of the puppet. Tell the class they will be using these stick puppets tomorrow.

3. Collect puppets.

Activity 4

1. Distribute stick puppets.

2. Explain to the children that you will tell them about some situations and you want them to hold up either the happy side or the sad side to show how the person might feel. Also point out that there are no right or wrong answers. It is important for the children to truthfully identify the feeling as they perceive it.

Situations:

- John gets a birthday present he likes.
- Sonya's favorite grandparent is coming to visit.
- Sonya's favorite grandparent's visit is over, and it's time for him/her to leave.
- Lee is going to the beach.

continued on next page

Grade Kindergarten • **skill** 1

- Kim is going grocery shopping with his father

- Jeremiah is raking leaves

- The coyote in a "Road Runner Cartoon" has just gotten blown up again.

3. Ask children to name other words for happy and sad. Make a chart, with a column for happy and a column for sad.

For example:

Happy	Sad
Joyful	Unhappy
Smiley	Droopy

You may want to leave room for additional columns for words such as angry or scared. Post the list next to the feeling words list from Day 2.

Although this activity does not specifically look at putdowns, at the end of each day's activity, ask students to listen and watch for putdowns so they can tell the class about them tomorrow.

Grade Kindergarten • **skill** 1

I Feel Angry

 Time Needed: 15 minutes

 Purpose: Students will identify anger as a reason people use putdowns.

Main Idea: We use putdowns when we are angry.

Materials: Picture book dealing with anger, chart paper and marker

Using This Activity

1. Explain to the class that you will be reading a story to them and you want them to pay special attention to the characters' feelings.

2. At appropriate stopping points, ask the class some of these questions: "What is the character feeling? [probably angry, mad, grouchy] What made him or her feel that way? How do we know what the character is feeling? What happened because the character was feeling that way?"

3. When you have finished reading and discussing the story, ask students to draw a picture about a time when they were angry.

4. Ask students, "Can you think of a time when feeling angry made you put someone down?"

Ask two or three students if they used or heard any putdowns, and invite them to tell the class about them. Caution them not to use the names of other people involved. Give appropriate feedback.

Book suggestions:
• *Benjamin and Tulip* by Rosemary Wells
• *All the Animals Were Angry* by William Wondriska
• *The Little Brute Family* by Russell Hoban
• *The Grouchy Ladybug* by Eric Carle
• *Spinky Sulks* by William Steig

◄ As a reading readiness exercise, write "I was angry when..." on the chalkboard. Call on students to complete that sentence.

You might also want to ask students for other words that mean angry. Write those words on chart paper and post it next to the other feelings lists, or add a column to the Happy/Sad Chart from Days 3-4.

Remind students to continue to pay attention to any putdowns they see or hear so they can report about them.

Sitting in the Scared Chair

Ask two or three students if they have used or heard any put-downs, and invite them to tell the class about them. Caution them not to use the names of other people involved. Give appropriate feedback.

 Time Needed: 30 minutes

 Purpose: Students will identify fear as a reason we use putdowns.

 Main Idea: We use putdowns when we are scared.

 Materials: Chair with word "scared" taped to it.

Using This Activity

1. Have the class sit in a circle.

You may want to start the activity by sitting in the chair yourself.

➤ **2.** Show the class the "scared chair" and explain that each child will sit in the chair and tell about a time when he/she felt scared. Encourage students to also say what happens to them when they are scared. For example, perhaps students cry, hide, get tough, or seek help. Ask students, "Can you think of a time when feeling scared made you put someone down or get angry with someone?"

Remind students to continue to pay attention to any putdowns they make.

Class Feelings Mural

 Time Needed: 5 minutes, introduction; ongoing during day.

 Purpose: Students will practice recognizing feelings.

 Main Idea: We can often tell how people feel just by looking at them.

 Materials: Photos of people from magazines and newspapers; crayons and markers; student family photos

Using This Activity

1. Stretch out a large roll of paper across a wall or bulletin board and within reach of children. Make four wide columns with a feeling word at the top of each: happy, sad, angry, scared.

2. Explain to the class that you will be asking them to help create a mural of feelings by taping photos under the appropriate column or drawing a feeling picture in one of the columns. This can be done throughout the day.

3. You might also talk briefly about how students can tell from a photo how someone feels. [They will probably answer that the person is smiling or frowning. They may also point out some body language or refer to the situation as being happy, sad, scary or angry.]

Ask students if they have used or heard any putdowns, and invite them to tell the class about them. Caution them not to use the names of other people involved. Give appropriate feedback.

◄ You may want to have children bring some family photos to school.

◄ Draw a feeling face next to each word.

◄ During the course of the day, while students are working independently, invite individuals to come up and place a feeling photo or draw a feeling picture under the column of their choice.

If this is set up as work stations, try to monitor the students and assess whether children can identify feelings.

Remind students to continue to pay attention to any putdowns they use or hear.

Feelings and Choices

Ask students if they have used or heard any putdowns, and invite them to tell the class about them. Caution them not to use the names of other people involved. Give appropriate feedback.

 Time Needed: 15 minutes

 Purpose: Students will label situations with a feeling (happy, sad, angry, scared, proud)

 Main Idea: Recognition of feelings is a step in beginning to deal with putdowns.

 Materials: Puppets

If puppets are not available, use stuffed animals, dolls, or even other children in role-play.

Using This Activity

1. Ask the class to form a circle. Explain that they will be doing some acting with the puppets. You will set the scene, and a child will use a puppet to respond.

Suggested situations:

Explain that when they feel happy, they get along with other people. If they are angry at one friend, though, they might take it out on lots of other people too. If they are happy, they may not get upset about a small problem or disappointment. But if they are already angry or sad about something, little disappointments or problems seem even bigger.

- The other person calls you a bad name.
- Nobody will play with you at recess.
- You are talking to your friend who has a broken arm.
- The teacher calls on you in class.
- Your friend just pushed you down.
- You had a nightmare last night.
- You are going to Disneyland tomorrow.
- Your teacher said, "That's great."
- You lost the game you were playing with a friend.

- Your friend told you that you did a good job.
- Your friend received a new toy and won't let you play with it.
- Your teacher didn't choose you for a game you wanted to play.
- It is Saturday.
- Your bike has a flat tire.
- Your pet died.
- You have the chicken pox.
- Your lunch money is missing.
- You won first place in a race.
- You have to go to the dentist.
- You hear thunder.

2. After each role-play, ask the rest of the class to identify the feeling the actors were showing: happy, sad, angry, scared (or other feeling words they have learned). Then ask the child who acted it out what he or she was feeling.

Remind students to continue to pay attention to any putdowns they use or hear.

The Three Little Pigs

Time Needed: 15 minutes

Purpose: Students will recognize and identify feelings through the use of literature.

Main Idea: A putdown can start a cycle of putdowns. A putdown may lead to an action which leads to another putdown.

Materials: None

Using This Activity

1. Explain the cycle of putdowns to the class: Feelings of fear, anger or unhappiness lead to putdowns, which lead to more upset feelings.

2. Ask for volunteers to act out the story of "The Three Little Pigs." This can be a spontaneous performance, no rehearsal necessary, but you may want to assign roles.

3. Explain to the rest of the class that their job is to be the audience. As the audience, they are to watch for feelings and identify any putdowns they hear or see.

Ask students if they have used any putdowns, and invite them to tell the class about them. Caution them not to use the names of other people involved. Give appropriate feedback.

◄ *Extending the Activity*
Point out to the class that sometimes people see the same event very differently. Then read *The True Story of the Three Pigs by A. Wolf* by Jon Scieszka.
After reading the story, ask children if they have a different opinion of the wolf and the pigs now. Do they think the pigs did anything to hurt the wolf's feelings or put him down?

Remind students to continue to pay attention to any putdowns they use or hear.

Use this wrap-up on the last day of the skill, even if you have not had time to work through all the activities.

Ask students if they have used or heard any putdowns, and invite them to tell the class about them. Caution them not to use the names of other people involved. Give appropriate feedback.

Skill Wrap-up

 Time Needed: 10-15 minutes

 Purpose: Students will review key concepts.

 Main Ideas: Putdowns are words or actions that hurt another person.
Putdowns are often caused by strong feelings.

 Materials: Index card sets.

Teacher Preparation:

Prepare several 16-card game sets for a word matching game. Each game set consists of four cards for each of the main feelings: happy, sad, angry, scared. Make four copies of the worksheet on the next page for each set needed.

Using This Activity

1. Ask students to name feelings again. The list may be longer than it was when you asked at the beginning of this skill.

2. Review the key concepts:

- Feelings are neutral. They are not good or bad. What counts is what we do when we are feeling that way.

- We are more likely to use putdowns when we are feeling sad, angry or scared.

- Putdowns hurt.

3. Tell students that they are going to play a matching game with feelings faces. Students can break into pairs or small groups to play this matching or memory game. Have them name the feeling as they make their matches.

At the end of this review, you may want to give a preview of the next skill. Simply announce, "Next week we'll start a new skill called 'Stay Cool.' We'll learn more about how to stay calm even if we are upset."

Happy

Scared

Sad

Angry

SKILL EVALUATION

Please complete this brief evaluation at the conclusion of your work on this skill.

1.   Activities in this skill which worked well for me were:

2.   Activities in this skill which were meaningful to my class were:

3.   Activities which needed adjustments were:

4.   I was unable to complete the following lessons in the two week instructional period:

5.   Ways in which I can include those lessons in my plans for the remainder of the year:

6.   Ways to improve this unit for future *No Putdowns* work are:

SKILL 2

Stay Cool

**A Program for Creating a Healthy
Learning Environment by Encouraging,
Understanding and Respecting**

Introduction to Stay Cool

This skill, "Stay Cool," is about learning to manage feelings. We do not have to be at the mercy of our feelings. We can recognize, own and manage feelings, and these skills can be taught.

Practice, practice, and more practice, along with instruction and reinforcement, are the keys to this skill.

Use opportunities during the day to reinforce this skill. The most vital teaching can happen in "real life." During the next two weeks, ask students if they are practicing the "Stay Cool" strategies at home or on the playground. If a "teachable moment" presents itself and a student is upset, ask what "Stay Cool" strategy to use. Point out when you notice a student staying cool. If a situation got out of control, talk about ways the participants could have stayed cool. Focus on what can be improved, not what has gone wrong.

Getting angry is perfectly normal and healthy. But the way anger is expressed can lead to trouble. This can be a difficult concept for children—and some adults! If possible, help children think about what they do when they get angry. Explain that it is okay to be angry, but it is not okay to express it by breaking things, hitting people, or putting down others.

These tricks may seem funny or awkward to the class at first, but they can help students get through difficult situations. These techniques won't work all the time, but they can be very useful in "buying some time" to think about what has happened before responding.

 Time Needed: 10 minutes

 Purpose: Students will be introduced to the skill of staying cool.

 Main Idea: We can learn ways to calm down when we are angry or upset.

Materials: None

Using This Activity

1. Briefly review Skill 1, "Think About Why," in which the class learned about identifying feelings.

2. Explain that strong feelings, especially anger and fear, are sometimes hard to handle. Sometimes we get so angry and upset that we can't think clearly and we do things that are not appropriate. For the next two weeks, the class will be talking about a new skill, "Stay Cool." They will learn ways to calm down so that they don't express their anger in harmful ways.

3. Ask students to tell about times when they felt "out of control." What happened when they got very angry? How did they show that they were angry? How did their parents, friends, etc. react? Did the way they expressed their anger lead to more conflict?

4. Remind students that starting tomorrow, they will be learning some "tricks" for managing their feelings.

Corduroy Discussion

 Time Needed: 20 minutes

 Purpose: Students will recognize there are strategies to use when they are troubled or angry.

 Main Idea: There are many ways to deal with feelings.

 Materials: *Corduroy* by Don Freeman; class bear (or other class mascot)

Synopsis of story:

Corduroy, a stuffed bear, would desperately like a home. A little girl sees him in the store and wants to buy him. Her mother won't buy him for her, but the little girl finds a way to buy Corduroy herself.

Using This Activity

1. Introduce the class bear or other stuffed animal or mascot. Read *Corduroy* to the class. As you read, stop and ask the children what they think the characters are feeling.

2. When you finish reading the book, help the class talk about times when they felt the same way as Corduroy or the little girl. Ask, "What would you have done — or what have you done when you haven't gotten what you wanted? What do you say when an adult says 'No?' "

3. Ask students to talk about how the little girl handled the situation when her mother said she couldn't have Corduroy. Ask, "Did she get angry?" Help the class see that the little girl went home and figured out how to solve the problem of wanting the bear. Help your students see that they have choices about how to deal with a problem.

The class bear or animal is not essential for the activity, but it can be helpful for this and subsequent activities. If you have a puppet or stuffed animal with which the class is familiar, use that. This "friend" will help the students learn and practice their new skills.

Counting to Ten

Counting is a simple strategy that anyone can use any time or any place.

You can also demonstrate this strategy using your class bear or class mascot. Pretend the stuffed animal is getting angry, and show how it stopped itself and counted to ten.

Relate the need for practice to activities the children are learning. Explain that using this strategy takes practice.

 Time Needed: 10 minutes

 Purpose: Students will count to ten as a strategy to "Stay Cool."

Main Idea: Counting silently or aloud helps some people calm down.

Materials: Ten manipulative counting objects for each child

Using This Activity

1. Explain that today the class will learn a strategy for staying cool — counting to ten. They can use this strategy any time they get mad—at school or home, on the bus or the playground. It may work better for some people than others, but with practice, everyone can do it.

2. Provide each student with a set of ten manipulative objects.

3. Lead the class in counting aloud to ten by setting out the objects one by one.

4. Have students practice counting to themselves using the objects.

5. Have students put the objects aside and practice counting to ten aloud and then to themselves.

6. Remind students that any time they are upset, they can count to ten to themselves to calm down and—STAY COOL.

Take Deep Breaths

 Time Needed: 10 minutes

 Purpose: Students will learn to take a deep breath as a calming strategy.

Main Idea: Deep breaths help people relax when they are tense.

Materials: Class bear or other stuffed animal or puppet

Using This Activity

1. Review yesterday's strategy: Counting to Ten.

2. Introduce another strategy for staying cool — Take Deep Breaths. Explain that deep breathing helps us relax our minds and our bodies. We can make a decision to take three or four deep breaths when we feel angry.

3. Demonstrate what you mean by slowly inhaling, then slowly exhaling.

4. Ask students to spread out around the class. As they stand, have them practice deep breathing. Keep reminding them to inhale deeply and slowly and to exhale smoothly and slowly.

◄ As a guideline, silently count to three as you inhale and then count to three as you exhale. You may want to tell your class to count slowly to themselves as they practice, or you can count aloud for them.

◄ Some students may try to hold their breath instead of letting it out slowly. Point out that holding one's breath causes tightness and tension—the opposite of calming down.

Freeze Please

The Freeze Please strategy works well in combination with counting to ten or deep breathing. After "freezing," the children may take a moment to count or breathe deeply to focus their thoughts.

 Time Needed: 15 minutes

 Purpose: Students will learn to stop or freeze when they need to calm themselves.

Main Idea: When you feel angry or frustrated, stop a moment to keep trouble from escalating.

 Materials: Music, class animal

Using This Activity

1. Briefly review the two previous "Stay Cool" strategies: Count to Ten and Take Deep Breaths. Then tell the class you are going to teach them another way to stay cool.

2. Explain that they will be playing a game something like Musical Chairs. As you play music, the children will move around the room. When you stop the music, you will say "Freeze Please" and the children must stop in place. Stop and start the music several times so they can practice "freezing."

As you act out the scenario, show the bear getting upset. For example, the bear may reach for the classmate's painting to rip it. But before he can, the class reminds him to "Freeze Please." This strategy, like the others, is not encouraging children to bury their feelings of anger. It is simply a way to "buy time" and think about their next move, to choose to tell the other person, "I'm angry," rather than automatically reacting. In Skill 4, "Choose a Response," there will be more discussion about what to do after cooling off.

3. Have students sit at their desks. Demonstrate the Freeze Please strategy by acting out a few scenarios in which the class bear (or other animal or puppet) is getting angry because:

• Someone tells the bear its painting is ugly.

• Someone takes the bear's truck.

• Someone scribbles on the bear's paper.

4. Each time the bear starts to get very angry, have the class tell the bear to "Freeze Please."

5. Once again explain that freezing gives us a chance to calm down and think before we get too angry and out of control. When we get out of control, we often say or do things that are hurtful to ourselves or others.

Grade Kindergarten • **skill** 2

Hot and Cold

 Time Needed: 10-20 minutes

 Purpose: Students will learn that "Stay Cool" means keep calm.

Main Idea: Hot and cold are words associated with actions and feelings as well as temperature.

Materials: Object to hide

Using This Activity

1. Explain that you will be playing the "Hot and Cold Game." The child who is "It" will look for the hidden object. The class will help by giving temperature readings: from cold to very hot. Cold means the child is way off track, warm means headed in the right direction, hot means very close, etc.

2. Choose a child to be "It." Send him or her out of the room.

3. Ask another child to hide an object in the room.

4. Bring the child who is "It" back into the room. Keep playing until the child finds the object. Repeat as time allows with another child as "It."

5. After the class has settled down, discuss some of your observations:

- Point out how excited the kids got when the searcher was closer to the object—when he/she was "hot." Explain that "hot" is another word for angry and that hot made them excited.

- Point out how they became calmer as the searcher got "cooler" or "cold" (farther from the object). Explain that cool is another word for calm.

- Getting "hot" can get them closer to trouble. Staying "cool" can keep them away from trouble.

Extending the Activity

Lead the class in saying, "Stay Cool" loudly, then more and more softly until finally they are saying it silently. Explain that whispering or saying to ourselves, "Stay Cool," can also help us calm down.

Staying Still

 Time Needed: 10-15 minutes

 Purpose: Students will experience the state of being still.

 Main Idea: Staying cool or calm can feel peaceful, and it can be affected by surroundings.

 Materials: None

Using This Activity

1. Explain that staying cool can feel very peaceful. Challenge the class to a "staying still contest." Who can sit quietly for the longest amount of time? Remind the class to breathe slowly and deeply so that they will feel calm.

(Gradually, wiggling, whispering, etc. will start to escalate.) Use your judgment to decide when to call a halt to the contest.

2. Discuss the experience with the class. Point out that it is probably easier to stay quiet and still when others are also quiet and still. Was it harder to sit still as classmates returned to more active levels? Did it feel funny to try to sit still? What did your body feel like as you sat still?

You might also compare this process to a chain-of-events story that you have read to them, such as *The House That Jack Built; Buzz, Buzz, Buzz; A Fly Went By.*

➤ **3.** Explain that it is easier to stay calm if others are calm, and when one person gets upset, others are more likely to get upset.

Teddy Bear Puzzle

 Time Needed: Ongoing throughout the day, with 5 minutes for introduction and 5 minutes for closure

 Purpose: Students will practice "Stay Cool" strategies.

Main Idea: "Stay Cool" strategies can be practiced and observed.

Materials: Teddy Bear puzzle pieces, tape

Teacher Preparation

Make two copies of the bear provided on the next page. Post one copy on a bulletin board. Cut the other into eight to ten pieces.

Using This Activity

1. Challenge the class to name the "Stay Cool" strategies and then to remember to use them if they are getting frustrated or angry.

2. Explain that you will tape up a piece of the puzzle each time you notice someone using one of the "Stay Cool" strategies. Ask the children to watch for "Stay Cool" strategies too. If they see someone use a strategy, or if they used one and you didn't notice, ask them to tell you.

3. At the end of the day, point out how much of the bear puzzle was completed. If it wasn't completed, was it because the children were calm most of the day and did not need to use "Stay Cool" methods? Or did they forget to use them when they were upset?

 "Stay Cool" strategies
- Count to ten
- Take a deep breath
- Freeze
- Whisper, "Stay cool"

Cartoon Cool

Children can get very excited talking about their favorite television shows. If they get too rambunctious, take a moment to practice the "Stay Cool" strategies until they calm down.

 Time Needed: 15-20 minutes

 Purpose: Students will identify consequences of not staying cool.

Main Idea: Although many characters on popular television shows lose their cool, there are rarely consequences for their actions.

Materials: Chart paper

Using This Activity

1. Ask students to name their favorite television shows. List them on the board.

2. Ask about the characters in those shows: Do they ever lose their cool? How can you tell? What happens when they lose their cool? Through discussion, make the point that there are usually few negative consequences to their bad behavior.

3. Ask if this lack of consequences is true in real life. What happens if you hit someone? What happens if you call someone else a name?

Often in cartoons and other television shows or movies, there are few consequences when a character gets angry. In cartoons, characters are not hurt even when blown up with dynamite or pushed off a cliff. In many other shows, there are no consequences—punishment or hurt feelings—when someone is mean to another character.

If most of your students watch only educational programming, ask them instead to talk about how the characters on their favorite shows stay cool and how they treat each other in positive and respectful ways.

Skill Wrap-up

 Time Needed: 25 minutes

 Purpose: Students will make personal fans.

 Main Idea: We can use fans as reminders to stay cool.

 Materials: Construction paper, art materials (optional: frozen treat sticks)

Using This Activity

1. Review the main reason for staying cool: to buy time to think clearly. Then ask children to name or demonstrate the strategies: count to ten, breathe deeply, say or whisper, "Freeze please," whisper, "Stay cool."

2. Distribute materials so that children can make fans. The fans can be either accordion-pleated or a circle with a stick attached to the back.

3. Instruct students to decorate their fans with reminders to stay cool.

4. Have students take the fans home to explain the skill to their parents.

It is extremely important to establish a link with parents regarding *No Putdowns*. The more practice, modeling and reinforcement the students are involved in, the higher the chance for success in reducing putdowns.

SKILL EVALUATION

Please complete this brief evaluation at the conclusion of your work on this skill.

1.   Activities in this skill which worked well for me were:

2.   Activities in this skill which were meaningful to my class were:

3.   Activities which needed adjustments were:

4.   I was unable to complete the following lessons in the two week instructional period:

5.   Ways in which I can include those lessons in my plans for the remainder of the year:

6.   Ways to improve this unit for future *No Putdowns* work are:

GRADE
K

SKILL 3

Shield Myself

**A Program for Creating a Healthy
Learning Environment by Encouraging,
Understanding and Respecting**

Use teachable moments to reinforce this skill. If a situation arises, ask students for "Shield Myself" suggestions. Or say, "I noticed that so-and-so did . . . That was a good 'Shield Myself' strategy." Or discuss the situation that occurred. Ask what could have been done so that the children involved didn't end up feeling so upset.

Introduction to Shield Myself

Time Needed: 15 minutes

Purpose: Students will be introduced to the "Shield Myself" skill.

Main Idea: We can protect ourselves from putdowns by recognizing our own strengths.

Materials: None

Using This Activity

1. Review the first two skills: "Think About Why" and "Stay Cool."

2. Explain that in the "Shield Myself" skill, students will be spending the next two weeks looking at themselves. "Shield Myself" is about self-esteem, recognizing our strengths and forming a positive self-image. By feeling good about ourselves, we can keep putdowns from seriously hurting us. A putdown does not change who we are.

Many teachers have used a Hula Hoop™ in "Shield Myself" as an image of the personal "safety zone." The hoop symbolizes our boundaries against putdowns. It is up to each of us to fill up the space inside with positive thoughts and beliefs about ourselves as a defense against being hurt.

3. Ask a few students to name a positive trait about themselves — something they do well, a quality they like about themselves, or an accomplishment of which they are proud. Explain that we all need to be able to name things we like about ourselves — and we all have a lot to be proud of. We all have special strengths and talents, and we need to discover them.

"All About Me" Booklets

 Time Needed: 30 minutes each activity

 Purpose: Students will create books about themselves.

 Main Idea: Each person has important characteristics and accomplishments to share.

Materials: Work pages (provided), crayons or markers, staples or yarn, construction paper

Using This Activity

Activities 2-6

Each day, distribute a work page to the students. Instruct them to illustrate the page so that it is personal to them:

    a. Things I Can Do

    b. Things That Make Me Feel Good

    c. Family and Friends

    d. Marvelous Me

    e. Places I Like to Go

Activity 7

On this last day, students will make a cover for their booklets, using construction paper and other art supplies, and assemble them using staples, yarn or ribbon.

For kindergarten, the core of "Shield Myself" is creation of the "All About Me" booklets in which children focus on their accomplishments. Recognizing one's uniqueness is important for many reasons:

• When students hear put-downs, they can begin to balance them with what they know to be true about themselves.

• Recognizing strengths breeds confidence, which helps weaken the impact of put-downs.

• Accomplishments encourage people to try more things.

If possible, take a few minutes each day to allow students to share their drawings with other students. If time allows, students can dictate labels or sentences to be written under their drawings.

Students could also create covers on a computer and print them out on colored paper.

THINGS I CAN DO

THINGS THAT MAKE ME FEEL GOOD

Marvelous Me

Grade Kindergarten • **skill** 3

PLACES 1 LIKE TO VISIT

I Am Special

This activity can be a very powerful and moving experience for students of any age. It is a clear demonstration of what can happen when putdowns are constantly present.

 Time Needed: 20 minutes

 Purpose: Students will recognize that one's self-concept can be destroyed by putdowns.

Main Idea: There are constant attacks on an individual's self-concept.

Materials: Class bear or animal (see Skill 2), heart-shaped paper sign with words "I Am Special"

Using This Activity

1. As preparation for this activity, cut out a paper heart, and write the words "I AM SPECIAL" in large, bold print.

2. Hold the I AM SPECIAL heart to your chest so that everyone can see it, and explain, "Everyone carries an invisible I AM SPECIAL sign around with them all the time, wherever they go. This is our *self-concept*. Self-concept is how we feel about ourselves. But the condition of our sign—how good we feel about ourselves—is affected by how others treat us. If somebody is nasty to us or teases us, puts us down, or hits us, then a piece of our I AM SPECIAL sign is destroyed." [Illustrate this concept by tearing a piece off of the sign.]

3. Tell the children that you are going to tell them a story about how this happens in everyday life. An outline is provided below. Each time an event negatively affects the hero of the story, tear another piece from the I AM SPECIAL sign until, at the end, you are left with almost nothing. Feel free to embellish or change the story provided, or create your own story.

A kindergarten bear named (your class bear's name) is still in bed three minutes after the alarm goes off. Mom yells upstairs, "_____, you are so lazy. Can't you do anything for yourself? Get your body out of bed and down here before I have to come up there and get you out of bed." [Rip a piece of the sign.]

Bear gets out of bed and starts to get dressed but can't find any clean socks. He asks Mom, but Mom says, "It's your own fault. If you wouldn't be so lazy and thoughtless and would put your dirty clothes in the laundry like I told you...(Roll eyes and act disgusted) Just wear yesterday's smelly socks." [Rip]

The pieces that are ripped today will be reconstructed tomorrow, so don't make them too tiny or fragile.

He goes to brush his teeth, but big sister is already in the bathroom and says, "Get lost, you little creep."

When Bear goes down to breakfast, the cereal is already soggy. Mom says, "It's your own fault. If you would get up on time, your cereal wouldn't be mush by the time you got down here. Eat it anyway. It's what you deserve." [Rip] As Bear leaves for school, Mom calls out, 'You've forgotten your lunch. You'd forget your head if it wasn't attached. Why can't you be more like your sister?" [Rip]

Bear has to run to catch the school bus, and when he gets on, the bus driver snarls, "Hurry up, kid, I don't have all day. Do you think I'll wait just for you? You think you're that important?" [Rip]

Once bear gets to school, the day doesn't go any better. During art class, someone calls his drawing ugly. [Rip] When Bear builds a tower, someone purposely knocks it over. [Rip] At lunch, someone cuts in line in front of Bear and refuses to move. [Rip]

After school, Bear's father gets angry about a bad grade on a spelling test and says, "Why can't you be smart like your sister?" [Rip]

Bear's day just went on and on like this, and it practically ended the same way it began. When Bear finished his homework, he started to work on a drawing and didn't hear his father tell him to get ready for bed. His father yelled at him, "You get up to bed NOW. Can't you ever get yourself to bed on time without my yelling at you?" [Rip]

When he got in bed, his mother turned the light out—and she didn't kiss him like she usually did. [Rip] Bear pulled the covers over his head and whispered to himself, "I can't do anything right." [Rip]

4. After you finish telling the story, ask the children if they think Bear felt very special anymore. What has happened to Bear's I AM SPECIAL sign?

5. Reassure the students that Bear will have a better day tomorrow, and that they will help build him up again. [Save the pieces of the heart for the following activity.]

Children may not consider all of the actions to be hurtful. They are simply illustrations of the way small hurts can accumulate and over time destroy our confidence, enthusiasm and will.

Explain that in the next *No Putdowns* skill, the class will talk about ways that Bear or anybody can respond to putdowns and not just feel sad.

Rebuilding Bear's Heart

Time Needed: 20 minutes

Purpose: Students will examine ways in which they can shield themselves.

Main Idea: When children hear putdowns, they can practice ways to protect themselves.

Materials: Class bear, paper heart pieces from previous day, pins or tape

Using This Activity

1. Ask the children for suggestions of ways to shield themselves. Help them to make a list. ◄

2. Ask them to name things that Bear could do to help rebuild his heart.

3. Tell about Bear's day again, but this time, ask the class to help Bear shield himself. Each time Bear shields himself, pin or tape another piece of the heart back together. ◄

4. Point out that with confidence, self-discipline and self-esteem, we can rebuild our I AM SPECIAL signs and our self-concept.

"Shield Myself" strategies include:

- Think positive things about yourself. (I can do this. I am good at drawing.)
- Respond to negative comments. (I am not a little creep.)
- Ask questions. (Why did you say that? Mom, why did you forget to kiss me good night?)
- Keep trying. (I'll try to be on time next time.)
- Be confident.

You may want to talk to the class about the "rebuilt" heart. Ask how the heart looks now. What do students notice about it in comparison to when you first held it up? The heart is taped back together, but it has scars. Point out that although we can rebuild our I AM SPECIAL signs, all the hurts and putdowns leave scars. We can feel good about ourselves again, but some of those nasty comments stay with us in our memories and may even hurt again if we think about them. Our hearts are healed, but our I AM SPECIAL signs have been damaged.

Skill Wrap-up

 Time Needed: 15 minutes

 Purpose: Students will review key concepts of "Shield Myself."

 Main Idea: Everyone hears putdowns but there are ways to keep them from being too harmful.

Materials: None

Using This Activity

1. Review this skill by asking the class what they have learned in "Shield Myself." Ask what they learned about themselves. If they do not bring out the main points, steer the discussion toward the value of self-concept in protecting ourselves against putdowns.

2. If possible, point out situations that occurred in class in the past two weeks that will illustrate the value of this skill in keeping putdowns or hurts from destroying self-concept.

3. Announce that next week you will start a new skill, "Choose a Response," which will help students make choices about what to do in difficult situations.

Point out that people who have a good self-concept and who know how to shield themselves may receive fewer putdowns.

SKILL EVALUATION

Please complete this brief evaluation at the conclusion of your work on this skill.

1. Activities in this skill which worked well for me were:

2. Activities in this skill which were meaningful to my class were:

3. Activities which needed adjustments were:

4. I was unable to complete the following lessons in the two week instructional period:

5. Ways in which I can include those lessons in my plans for the remainder of the year:

6. Ways to improve this unit for future *No Putdowns* work are:

GRADE
K

SKILL 4

Choose a Response

**A Program for Creating a Healthy
Learning Environment by Encouraging,
Understanding and Respecting**

Introduction to Choose a Response

"Choose a Response" address-es the choices of what to do when scared, angry or frustrat-ed or if someone has made a putdown. What can a child do instead of using a putdown in retaliation? Many children and adults think that they are at the mercy of their feelings and have no control or choice about how they respond. They "automati-cally" use a putdown or wise-crack, yell or make threats. Others bite their tongues and say nothing and let hurts eat away at them. This fourth skill is designed to help children see that they have many choices about how to respond to a diffi-cult situation.

At this level, you can use a very simple definition of conflict such as, "when people are not get-ting along." You might also ask for other words for conflict. Children may respond with words such as fight, argument, disagreement, yelling, pushing or not sharing.

Possible responses to a putdown or other conflict fall into two broad categories: talk it out and let it drop. Talking it out may mean talking to the person involved or talking it over with a third party. For the next two weeks, you will be exploring these options with your students.

 Time Needed: 5-10 minutes

 Purpose: Students will be introduced to Skill 4, "Choose a Response."

Main Idea: Everyone has choices when faced with daily sit-uations.

Materials: None

Using This Activity

1. Review the "Stay Cool" choices: Counting to Ten, Taking Deep Breaths, Saying, "Freeze please," or whispering, "Stay cool" to your-self. Explain that now it is time to talk about what to do after you have calmed down a little.

2. Ask if anyone knows what the word "conflict" means.

3. Ask students to tell you about conflicts or disagreements in which they have been involved. You may have to give some examples to get them started: wanting something that someone else is playing with; competing with a brother or sister for an adult's attention; call-ing someone a name; not letting someone play.

4. After taking several examples from the class, simply explain that conflicts can be large or small. They happen when people have dif-ferent ideas about what should be happening.

5. Ask what has happened as a result of some of the conflicts they named. Were they physically hurt? Did their feelings get hurt? Did they get into trouble with friends or parents?

6. Introduce the name of this fourth skill: "Choose a Response." Tell the class: For the next two weeks, we will look at ways to handle conflicts. We can choose how to behave when things don't go our way or when we are involved in a difficult situation.

Tell Them to Stop

Time Needed: 20 minutes

Purpose: Students will learn to ask someone to stop putting them down.

Main Idea: Saying "Stop" is one way to deal with putdowns.

Materials: None

Using This Activity

1. Explain that there are many choices we can make when someone is bothering us or putting us down. One of those choices is to "Tell them to stop." Explain that this is a way to let the other person know that you don't like what they are saying or doing.

2. Ask children to tell you ways they could tell someone to stop. Write their responses on the board. ◄

3. Ask children to choose which responses are most likely to help and which may make the situation worse. Point out that they are trying to let the other person know, "I don't like what you are saying, and I would like you to stop."

4. Allow children time to practice this skill by arranging them in a circle for role-plays. Demonstrate the first role-play for them in the center of the circle. Choose a child from the circle to participate with you. Possible scenarios: ◄

   • Someone is poking you from behind in the lunch line.
   • Your little sister or brother is pestering you.
   • A classmate tries to grab a toy away from you.

5. After demonstrating one role-play, ask pairs of children to come to the center of the circle and practice telling someone else to "Stop please." Remind them to use a "Stop" statement that will help, not make the situation worse. Allow classmates to help if the pair seems to be struggling.

Not all strategies will work all the time. It is important to let children know that telling someone to stop may not always get them to stop!

Some of the ways children may name are:
• "Stop it!"
• "I don't like what you are saying to me."
• "You're bothering me."
• "Cut it out." At this point, don't comment on their suggestions, even if their way of saying "stop" seems inappropriate.

Don't hesitate to use the *No Putdowns* framework when dealing with classroom or individual situations. Practice is the key to this skill.
If possible, role play situations that have actually occurred in your classroom, on the bus, in the halls, and on the playground. You might also use home situations that you have heard the children discussing.

Walk Away

The three strategies are being presented in the order in which a child might try them in a situation. A first response might be "Tell them to stop." If that doesn't work, a child can "Walk away." If the situation continues, the child might seek out an adult (see Day 4).

 Time Needed: 15 minutes

 Purpose: Students will learn that walking away is a choice to make when faced with a putdown.

 Main Idea: Sometimes, but not always, it is appropriate to walk away.

Materials: None

A child may suggest that walking away is like running away and being a coward. Explain the difference between choosing to walk away and running away in fear. Walking away is a choice.

Using This Activity

1. Review the first strategy, "Tell them to stop." Then tell the class that you are going to teach them another way to handle a situation when someone is putting them down. It is also a good strategy for children to use if they are getting angry and need to stay cool.

You may need to clarify the point about not walking away from teachers, parents and other adults. Children need to know to walk away if approached by a stranger or if they feel endangered by an adult they know.

2. Introduce this strategy called "Walk away." It simply means walking away from a bad situation. Explain that this does not mean "walk away" from a parent or teacher who is talking to you.

To make this activity more interesting and to appeal to kinesthetic learners, you may want to have children spread out around the classroom. After you read a scenario, have children either stay in place or tiptoe away. Give them a signal to stop tiptoeing after they have taken a few steps.

3. Ask children to tell you which of these situations might be a good time to "walk away":

- A friend is calling you names.

- Your mother is scolding you for spraying your brother with a hose.

- The other kids in the neighborhood said you are too little to play with them.

- The teacher told you to stop running in the hall.

4. Review both strategies: "Tell them to stop" and "Walk away."

ACTIVITY 4

Tell an Adult

 Time Needed: 25 minutes

 Purpose: Students will learn they can go to an adult for help in a confrontation.

Main Idea: Sometimes a child needs to seek the help of an adult in handling a situation.

Materials: Paper, crayons or markers

Using This Activity

1. Explain to the children that another response to a putdown situation is "Tell an adult." Give examples of situations in which this strategy might be a good idea:

   • You or someone else is in danger.

   • A bully has been harassing you repeatedly.

   • All other efforts have not been successful.

   Caution the children that often they should try "Tell them to stop" or "Walk away" before they try "Tell an adult."

2. Instruct students to draw a picture of a time when telling an adult was a good idea.

3. Help students write a descriptive sentence at the bottom of their pictures.

Some children might be concerned that they are being tattletales. Discuss when "telling" is appropriate. Point out that "tattling" means telling on someone just to get her in trouble. Telling an adult in the context of *No Putdowns* means going to an adult because you have tried the appropriate choices and they haven't worked. Point out that many situations will be resolved by telling them to stop or by walking away.

Which Response?

 Time Needed: 15-20 minutes each activity

 Purpose: Students will practice choosing responses.

 Main Idea: We always have choices.

 Materials: Chart paper, stick-up notes or slips of paper, tape

Teacher Preparation:

Write up slips of paper with conflict situations appropriate to kindergarten children. Try to create situations that happen in your classroom, or on the bus or playground. Fold up the slips of paper and put them into a box. You should create enough for the entire class to have a turn.

On large chart paper, make three columns with these headings:

Stop	Walk	Tell

Using This Activity

1. Ask for a volunteer to draw a slip of paper from the box.

2. Help the student read aloud the situation on the slip. Then ask her to tell you which of the three strategies she would use: "Tell them to stop" (column 1), "Walk away" (column 2) or "Tell an adult" (column 3).

3. After the student has chosen a strategy, have her attach the slip of paper under the appropriate column.

4. Repeat this process until all children have had a turn.

This activity may take two days to get through the entire class. Scenarios do not all have to be simple or clear-cut.

For example:

- *Another child has called you a name.*
- *Another child keeps calling you names even though you have already told him to stop.*
- *Another child pushed you down, and you come home with your clothes torn.*
- *You were pushed on the bus steps.*
- *Your good friend won't let you play with him.*
- *Your friend broke your crayon.*
- *A big kid laughed at your coat.*
- *Your sister kicked you.*

As part of each child's turn, you may want to ask for more information beyond the strategy she would choose. If the child selects "Stop," you might ask how that request could be worded. If the child chooses "Tell an adult," what would she say?

ACTIVITY 7

Finish These Poems

Time Needed: 15 minutes

Purpose: Students will learn rhymes describing "Choose a Response" skills.

Main Idea: There are many possible responses to a situation.

Materials: Rhythm instruments

Using This Activity

1. These rhyme completions can be done individually or as a group. Ask children to finish these rhymes by filling in one of the three strategies:

   a. When a kid says, "Your hair looks like a mop,"

      Just tell them, "I don't like your words, and _I want you to stop._"

   b. If the bigger kids won't let you play,

      Don't get in a fight, _Just walk away._

   c. If you have tried everything and can't fix it yourself,

      Don't stand there and yelp,

      Find an adult and ask for _help._

2. Lead the class in chanting these short poems, and even add percussion to the chants through clapping, tapping, drums, sticks, rattles and so on.

3. Lead the class in a final chant:

   "*No Putdowns*, pass it around. Pass it around, *No Putdowns*."

◄ See the *No Putdowns* video for a performance of the chant.

If you have a school assembly, you may want to have your class perform the chants with drumming, tapping, clapping and so on.

Spelling and Writing Practice

 Time Needed: 15 minutes

 Purpose: Students will review the responses they have learned.

Main Idea: There are many possible responses to a situation.

 Materials: Activity sheet on the next page

Using This Activity

1. Review the strategies.

2. Instruct students to complete the activity sheet by filling in the four-letter word that goes with each symbol on the sheet.

➤ **3.** Urge children to take the worksheets home and talk to their families about each strategy.

This activity offers another opportunity to reach out to families. Send the completed worksheets home with children. A cover letter explaining the worksheet can create a valuable link between home and school. Simply explain that the children have been learning three responses to putdown situations: Tell them to stop, Walk away, and Talk it out. Encourage parents to reinforce these responses at home.

Name_____

_ _ _ _ _ _ _

_ _ _ _ _ _ _

_ _ _ _ _ _ _

Choose a Response

What Will Happen?

 Time Needed: 20 minutes

 Purpose: Students will identify consequences of not using *No Putdowns* responses.

Main Idea: Actions have consequences, and we must choose which action to take in a situation.

Materials: Situation slips from Days 5 and 6, chart paper

Teacher Preparation:

Draw two columns on a sheet of chart paper with these headings:

If You Stop, Walk or Tell	If You Don't Stop, Walk or Tell

Using This Activity

1. Choose a situation slip of paper from Days 5 and 6 and read it aloud to the class.

2. Ask, "What could happen if you do use one of the *No Putdowns* responses?"
List their answers on the board.

3. Ask, "What could happen if you don't use the *No Putdowns* responses and just react?"

4. Ask which results sound more attractive.

5. Do this same activity with other situations as time allows. Or use incidents that have happened in the classroom in the past day or so as examples.

Some of the possible consequences of using the *No Putdowns* responses include:
You keep on playing
You are all happier
There is no trouble
You will still be friends
People don't get hurt

Possible consequences of not following the *No Putdowns* responses:
Crying
Broken things
You will lose a friend
People are hurt
The teacher gets angry

Skill Wrap-up

Time Needed: 15 minutes

Purpose: Students will create an ending to a story dealing with conflict.

Main Idea: There are many possible responses to a conflict.

Materials: Story opening provided below or a storybook of choice [should be one not familiar to the class], art supplies (optional)

Using This Activity

1. Read the story opening to the class:

◄ You can use the story started here, make up your own, or read the beginning of a storybook that sets out a conflict in the first few pages.

When little Henry got the hiccups, his stuffed animal friends, Vanilla, Chocolate and Strawberry, thought they had better figure out a way to stop those hiccups. Unfortunately, they all had very different ideas about how to cure them.

Vanilla, the polar bear, said in a loud whisper, so as not to wake Henry, "Let's just scare him!"

"That's a stupid idea," Chocolate, the seal, grumbled. "Let's wake him up and tell him to hold his breath."

Strawberry was jumping up and down on the bed by this time. "I can't believe the ridiculous things that come out of your mouths. Chocolate, you're just a dopey, droopy, rag of an animal. And as for you, Vanilla...."

Just then, Henry hiccuped hard and sent the three animals tumbling around the crib. "Well, I'm sick of you too," Chocolate said to Strawberry when the quake was over. "You think you're so great because you're nearly new and Henry hasn't chewed on you yet."

Henry hiccuped again, and Vanilla, Chocolate and Strawberry held on to the covers. "We have a problem here," Vanilla reminded the other two.

Their stories in Step 2 do not have to show the "Choose a Response" strategies initially. In fact, it may be more fun and challenging if they continue to build the conflict with nonproductive ways to respond and then look at the consequences to the characters. Eventually try to guide students to bring in the strategies that have been discussed.

2. Ask the class to write the rest of the story by asking different children to tell what happens next. Be sure to stress that their stories must address the conflict, and what happens next depends on how they respond to the conflict.

◄ As an alternative to group story writing, try these:
- Ask children to draw a picture of how the story might end.
- Divide students into small groups to act out possible story continuations.

Please complete this brief evaluation at the conclusion of your work on this skill.

1. Activities in this skill which worked well for me were:

2. Activities in this skill which were meaningful to my class were:

3. Activities which needed adjustments were:

4. I was unable to complete the following lessons in the two week instructional period:

5. Ways in which I can include those lessons in my plans for the remainder of the year:

6. Ways to improve this unit for future *No Putdowns* work are:

SKILL 5

Build Up

**A Program for Creating a Healthy
Learning Environment by Encouraging,
Understanding and Respecting**

"Build Up" transfers *No Putdowns* from a "skill" into daily practice. Up to this point in the program, kids have learned theoretically or academically to recognize and handle putdowns. But they need a lot of practice building up themselves and others since many children—and adults—find it easier to put down than to build up. Review the possible reasons for putdowns—habit, modeled behavior, anger, frustration, jealousy, etc. Many children do not know what to say in place of putdowns. Now is the time to focus and practice.

Introduction to Build Up

 Time Needed: 10 minutes

 Purpose: Students will be introduced to Skill 5, "Build Up"

 Main Idea: The opposite of put down is build up.

 Materials: None

Using This Activity

1. Explain to the class that for the next ten days, they are going to get a lot of practice learning to be good to themselves and each other. But they will be learning ways to think and behave their entire lives.

2. Review what they have covered in the previous four skills:

"Think About Why"

"Stay Cool"

"Shield Myself"

"Choose a Response"

3. Explain that "Build Up" teaches what to do in place of putting yourself or others down.

Fish Bulletin Board

Time Needed: 30 minutes

Purpose: Students will learn about recognizing differences and offering encouragement and compliments.

Main Idea: Differences are not good or bad; they are simply differences.

Materials: Construction paper, scissors, crayons or markers, tape or push pins

Using This Activity

1. Post a large piece of blue paper on the bulletin board. (This is the water!)

2. Instruct students to create and decorate fish on their own paper and then cut them out.

3. Have students pin or tape their fish onto the blue background.

4. Discuss all the different styles and types of fish. How are they alike? How are they different? Discuss the idea that all the different fish make up one community. Talk about the concept of differences. Point out that differences do not make someone else wrong—just different!

5. Ask children about differences they see among people regarding looks, likes and dislikes, families, and so on. Again stress that differences are not good or bad.

6. Ask the children to offer compliments about their classmates' fish. You may need to offer the first ones: "This one has pretty stripes. This one is an interesting shape."

Silent Encouragers

 Time Needed: 15 minutes

 Purpose: Students will identify nonverbal encouragers and choose one for their sign.

Main Idea: Classmates can support each other with nonverbal clues.

Materials: Chart or blackboard

Using This Activity

➤ **1.** Ask students to think of nonverbal ways to encourage each other (for example, a thumbs-up). List their suggestions on the board.

2. Explain that the class is to choose one of those signs to use whenever they want to encourage a classmate either in class, around school, or outside of school. Challenge them to use this sign at least once every day.

Students may list items, such as applause or foot stomping. Write those on the list. For the class sign, however, you may want to choose something that doesn't make noise! Silent encouragers include:
- Thumbs-up sign
- High five
- Okay sign with thumb and forefinger
- Hands clasped above head (like a boxing champ)
- Crossed fingers
- Peace sign

As a follow-up, ask students to tell the class about using the sign in a situation.

ACTIVITY 4

We Think You Can

This is a good exercise to do in physical education class. Be sure to be sensitive to children with physical limitations.

 Time Needed: 20 minutes

 Purpose: Students will have an opportunity to encourage others and to be encouraged.

Main Idea: An encouraging word can make a task seem easier to accomplish.

Materials: *The Little Engine That Could* by Watly Piper

Using This Activity

1. Read *The Little Engine That Could* aloud.

2. Ask student volunteers to perform one of these types of activities as the rest of the class chants, "We think you can, we think you can."

> Walking on a balance beam
>
> Walking with a beanbag on head
>
> Jumping jacks
>
> Bouncing a ball
>
> Twirling a hoop around the arm
>
> Hopping on one foot
>
> Three-legged race
>
> Wheelbarrow walk
>
> Relay

As an alternative, see whether putdowns and negative comments affect children's ability to do the task. Have the class chant, "We think you can't, we think you can't." Have the children discuss how they felt when they were cheered on and how they felt when the class put them down.

These last three activities offer an opportunity for children to work cooperatively.

Grade Kindergarten • **skill** 5

This activity helps children learn to appreciate what other people do and to move away from the egocentrism of kindergartners! You might also want to talk about the school as a community of people working — and playing — together.

Touring the School

 Time Needed: 15-25 minutes

 Purpose: Students will observe positive circumstances happening in school.

Main Idea: Make a point of noticing the good things others do.

 Materials: None

Using This Activity

1. Take students on a walking tour of the school. Ask them to be on the watch for what others are doing to make the school a pleasant place to be. (For example, a nurse helping someone, a cafeteria worker cleaning up after lunch, a teacher complimenting or helping a student, a student working with another student.)

2. When the class returns to the classroom, ask them to name what they saw by complimenting the people they observed. For example: "Mrs. X was really washing tables in the cafeteria. They were very clean." You might even want to invite some of the people into the classroom so the children can compliment them directly.

Compliment or Criticism?

 Time Needed: 15 minutes

 Purpose: Students wil learn to respond in an encouraging or supportive manner.

Main Idea: Many situations have several responses, but practice choosing the supportive response.

Materials: None

Using This Activity

1. Present the following situations that could lead either to encouragement or putdowns. Ask students to tell how they could respond so that the other person feels supported and respected.

   a. You are working with another student, and she knocks the crayons over.

   b. You are playing a two-person game with another child, and a third child wants to join the game.

   c. Your best friend drops his bookbag in a puddle while you are waiting for the bus. The other kids laugh.

   d. Your little sister wants a toy you are playing with.

   e. Your teacher wants the class to settle down, but everyone is talking and running around.

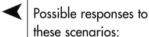 Possible responses to these scenarios:

a. Do you want me to help you pick them up?

b. Only two can play now, but you can play next time.

c. Offer to pick up the bookbag or hold other things so he or she can.

d. Offer another toy, or offer to let her use it a little later.

e. Settle down, and don't keep things going.

Language Experience Stories

 Time Needed: 20-25 minutes

 Purpose: Students will continue the discussion of choosing a putdown or build-up response.

 Main Idea: We can choose whether to put down or build up.

Materials: Paper, markers or crayons

Using This Activity

1. Have children draw pictures of situations that could turn into put-down or build-up situations, as in the previous day's activity.

2. Ask students to write stories to accompany their pictures. You may choose to have children write the stories themselves or dictate stories to you.

Spider Web

 Time Needed: 15-20 minutes

 Purpose: Students will practice complimenting a class-mate.

Main Idea: With practice, we can learn to make build-up responses.

Materials: Ball of yarn

Using This Activity

1. Ask students to sit in a circle.

2. Explain that you will toss the ball to a student and give encouragement or a compliment to that student. That student will hold on to part of the yarn, throw the ball to another student and say something encouraging to him or her.

◀ Remind students to hold on to a part of the yarn as they toss the yarn to another student.

3. Continue tossing the ball of yarn around the circle until every student has caught it and received a build-up comment.

◀ As the "web" grows, it may become more and more difficult to figure out who has not caught the ball yet. Encourage students to use their observation skills.

4. After everyone is part of the web, challenge the class to unravel the web. It will take teamwork and patience.

Encouragement Bowl

 Time Needed: 5 minutes for introduction; ongoing throughout the day

 Purpose: Students will monitor the number of build ups during the day.

 Main Idea: It's fun to practice using and noticing build ups.

 Materials: Quantity of marbles or dry beans, large jar

Using This Activity

➤ **1.** Explain that you are challenging your class to fill the jar with compliments and encouraging comments. Each time they hear a positive comment or compliment, they can put a marble or bean into the jar. If they hear a putdown, they are to take a marble or bean out of the jar.

➤ **2.** Once the jar is filled, ask the office to announce it on the PA system and/or award the class a document or letter.

Beware of having the whole class respond to a single incident! Each build-up response can be counted only once.

The purpose of this activity is practice and recognition of skills, not reward. Students should not be making build-up responses simply to win a reward. Build ups should be sincere!

ACTIVITY 10

No Putdowns Party

 Time Needed: 30 minutes

 Purpose: Students will celebrate the work they have done in ten weeks of *No Putdowns*.

Main Idea: This is the completion of the formal instruction period, but the skills take a lifetime of practice.

Materials: Depends upon activity chosen

Using This Activity

1. Have a party! The class has just completed ten weeks of *No Putdowns*. Today is a day to celebrate, have fun, feel good about themselves and their classmates. Partying together is also an opportunity to build community and class goodwill.

2. Ask students to name a highlight of the program, something important they learned.

3. If it is not appropriate to have separate class activities, have a grade-level or even school-wide celebration. That might mean treats in the cafeteria, a storyteller, games, a song person, etc.

A school-wide or even grade-level celebration will take planning by teachers and parents, since parents are a part of the *No Putdowns* process.

If parents are not included in the celebration, notify them that the formal instruction period of the program has ended but the work is ongoing at home and school.

Another choice is to have a "commencement" ceremony with presentation of class certificates or other recognitions.

Please complete this brief evaluation at the conclusion of your work on this skill.

1. Activities in this skill which worked well for me were:

2. Activities in this skill which were meaningful to my class were:

3. Activities which needed adjustments were:

4. I was unable to complete the following lessons in the two week instructional period:

5. Ways in which I can include those lessons in my plans for the remainder of the year:

6. Ways to improve this unit for future *No Putdowns* work are:

GRADE
1

**A Program for Creating a Healthy
Learning Environment by Encouraging,
Understanding and Respecting**

SOCIAL COMPETENCY TABLE
Grade 1

| | NO PUTDOWNS SKILLS | | | | |
SOCIAL COMPETENCIES	Skill 1: Think About Why	Skill 2: Stay Cool	Skill 3: Shield Myself	Skill 4: Choose a Response	Skill 5: Build Up
Communication Skills	X	X	X	X	X
Empathy	X		X	X	X
Self-worth			X	X	X
Respect	X			X	X
Self-control		X	X	X	X
Community Building	X		X	X	X
Conflict Resolution				X	
Anger/Stress Management		X		X	
Problem-solving				X	X
Violence Prevention	X	X		X	X

GRADE 1 ACTIVITIES

GRADE
1

SKILL 1

Think About Why

A Program for Creating a Healthy Learning Environment by Encouraging, Understanding and Respecting

If most of your students participated in the *No Putdowns* program last year, treat this lesson as review rather than new information.

Introduction to *No Putdowns*

 Time Needed: 15 minutes

 Purpose: Students will be introduced to *No Putdowns* and Skill 1, "Think About Why."

 Main Ideas: The entire school is participating in this program.

Putdowns are words or actions that are disrespectful.

Putdowns are often caused by strong feelings.

Materials: None

Using This Activity

1. Bring the class together for a discussion.

2. Ask your class, "Has anyone ever hurt your feelings or said or done something that made you feel terrible?" [Students may talk about name calling, pushing, spanking, scolding, being yelled at, being teased, and so on.]

3. After they have responded, refer to the incidents dealing with name-calling, being ignored or excluded, teasing, and similar actions. Tell the class, "When someone makes fun of us or hurts our feelings, we call that a putdown."

4. Explain that the entire school is starting a ten-week project called *No Putdowns*. The goals for the school and the class are to try not to use putdowns and to learn how to respond if someone does use a putdown.

Putdowns are words or actions that are disrespectful to another person, place or thing. Putdowns are usually said or done for reasons of power, anger, fear, jealousy, habit, humor, frustration, or modeled behavior. See the teacher's introductory materials for a full discussion of putdowns.

5. Tell the class, "We're going to be learning five skills in the next ten weeks. The first one is called 'Think About Why.' This week and next week, we're going to do activities that help us identify putdowns and try to figure out the feelings that lead to putdowns."

6. Wrap up this introduction by asking, "Do you have any idea why you say mean things to your brothers, sisters or classmates?" [Children may answer that someone made them mad, they couldn't do something they wanted to do, or the other person had something they wanted.] Point out that they had strong feelings when they made the putdown, and strong feelings can cause people to react in a variety of ways. That is why the whole school is learning the *No Putdowns* skills. Everyone in the school will learn about ways to be in charge of their own feelings and to be respectful of others.

If the school is involved in other character education efforts, this is a good time to make the connection so that students see that *No Putdowns* is another piece of the puzzle of how to treat themselves and others.

Ask students to listen and watch for putdowns so they can tell the class about them tomorrow.

Feeling Words

At the beginning of each *No Putdowns* session, allow two or three students to talk about putdowns they have witnessed, used or received. Invite them to tell the class about the putdown, but caution them not to use the names of other people involved. If no one has an anecdote to report, commend the class on doing a good job. If putdowns are reported, briefly discuss what happened and what to do differently next time.

If you have class meetings, that is a good forum for conducting some *No Putdowns* activities.

Children may need to tell about an experience in order to name a feeling. To introduce words such as jealous, nervous, frustrated, impatient, excited or eager, you may want to ask leading questions: How do you feel if someone gets a toy you have been wanting? How do you feel right before you are about to perform for an audience? How do you think other people feel if they try to do something and keep making mistakes?

Try to incorporate these new feeling words into daily interactions: "You seem frustrated, Tanya. Are you feeling nervous, Larry?"

Ask students to listen and watch for putdowns so they can tell the class about them tomorrow.

Time Needed: 15 minutes

Purpose: Students will review feeling words and increase feelings vocabulary.

Main Idea: Besides feeling happy, sad, scared and angry, people also feel jealous, frustrated, impatient, nervous or eager. Our feelings affect how we treat other people.

Materials: Chart paper, markers

Using This Activity

➤ **1.** Say to the class, "You may have learned four basic feeling words in kindergarten: happy, sad, scared, angry." As you say each one, write it on the chart paper.

➤ **2.** Explain that they are now going to learn some other feeling words. Ask if they can think of other feelings. Write each new feeling word on the chart paper. Save or post the list for use later on in this skill.

3. Discuss which of these feelings might lead to putdowns, arguments, or disagreements.

ACTIVITY 3

Anger Masks

Time Needed: 30 minutes

Purpose: Students will show how anger looks.

Main Idea: We all have a distinct look when we are angry.

Materials: Crayons or markers, paper bags, scissors

Using This Activity

1. Distribute materials. Explain that students are to use the bags to make masks that show how their faces look when they are angry. Have them cut eyeholes before they begin drawing.

2. After masks have been illustrated, have students put their masks on and walk around the room to look at each other's angry faces.

3. As children circulate, ask them to tell each other some of the things that make them angry.

4. Have students return to their seats. Ask them to help you list words that mean angry (mad, furious, annoyed).

5. Ask students to talk about how they think their bodies look when they are angry. What body language tells people they are angry? ◀

At the beginning of each *No Putdowns* session, ask students to report on putdowns they have witnessed, used or received since yesterday's lesson. (See Day 2 note.)

Possible body language responses include: frowning, tight muscles, clenched fists, crossed arms. You might also want to discuss how other people seem to feel when the student is expressing anger. (Answers might incude frightened, amused, embarrassed, shocked.)

Ask students to listen and watch for putdowns so they can report to the class tomorrow. Announce that the class will be making noisemakers tomorrow, and ask students to bring in materials, such as small jars, milk cartons, marbles or paper clips. You may want to write a note to parents.

I Hear a Putdown

Before beginning this activity, ask students to report on putdowns they have witnessed, used, or received since yesterday's lesson.[See Day 2 note.]

Time Needed: Activity 4, 20-30 minutes to make an instrument; Activity 5, 20-30 minutes to read the story and discuss the activity

Purpose: Students will identify putdowns.

Main Idea: Putdowns occur in many circumstances.

Materials: Storybook or video with putdowns; items to make noisemakers such as empty milk cartons, paper cups, small jars and bottles, empty paper towel rolls, wax paper, pebbles, beans, marbles, crayon bits

Using This Activity

Activity 4

Have students make noisemakers using their own materials or items you have provided.

Activity 5

1. Read a story or show part of a video that contains putdowns. Instruct the class to make noise with their noisemakers each time they hear a putdown or hurtful words.

➤ **2.** Students will need a cool-down period after making noise. Ask how it felt to make noise in response to putdowns. Many students probably found it a relief to make noise. If so, point out that they can't take their noisemakers with them everywhere to drown out putdowns or let their feelings out. But maybe they can think about the noisemaker when someone puts them down or they feel stressed.

This visualization of the noisemaker is an early step in dealing with a putdown. In Skill 2, students will learn about calming down, and in Skill 4, they will learn about responses they can choose once they have calmed down.

Remind students to listen and watch for putdowns so they can report to the class tomorrow.

Ask children to bring a scarf for tomorrow's lesson, or write a note to parents.

ACTIVITY 6

Blindfold Activity

 Time Needed: 20-30 minutes

 Purpose: Students will work in pairs as they participate in a blindfold walk.

 Main Idea: Frustration or fear may lead to putdowns.

 **Materials:** Scarves or other blindfolds

Using This Activity

1. Pair off students.

2. Instruct students that one student will be the guide and the other will be blindfolded, then they will switch roles. Explain that the "seeing" partner will lead the blindfolded partner around the classroom and will warn him or her of any obstacles or other problems as necessary. The "seeing" partner is responsible for the other child's safety and well-being.

3. After a few minutes, have students switch roles and repeat the walk within the room.

4. Gather the class together. Ask children how they felt as the seeing partner and as the blindfolded partner. You may want to prompt them: Was anyone scared? frustrated? nervous? excited?

5. Relate the activity to putdowns by asking: Did you feel at any time that your partner put you down? Did you ever feel like putting your partner down?

Ask students to report on any putdowns they have witnessed, used or received since yesterday's lesson. [See Day 2 note.]

◄ Ask children to bring scarves or blindfolds from home, but have some extras on hand in case they forget.

◄ You may want to treat this activity as an opportunity to discuss sensitivity to differences, especially if there are children with visual or other impairments in your class.

Ask students to listen and watch for putdowns so they can tell the class about them tomorrow.

Feeling Word Pictures

Ask for student reports on putdowns witnessed or used since yesterday's lesson. [See Day 2 note.]

 Time Needed: 15 minutes

 Purpose: Students will identify nonverbal clues about feelings.

Main Idea: People communicate their feelings with their body language and facial expression.

Materials: Photos illustrating feeling words listed on class chart. [See Day 2 for chart.]

Using This Activity

Children will probably respond that the person is smiling or frowning. Point out any other clues, such as how the person is standing or sitting, or how they are looking at the other person.

1. Hold up each photo or illustration, and ask students to identify the main feeling of each person in it.

➤ 2. Ask how the class knew what the feeling was, even though no one was speaking. You might even ask, "What do you think this person would like to say to the other person in the picture — or to anyone who will listen?"

Ask students how they can tell when their parents are angry. You may want to discuss tone of voice at this point. Demonstrate how the same sentence can have different meanings depending on how you say it. Use comments or requests that you use often in the classroom: "Quiet down, bring me your paper, line up for lunch, nice job." Say each phrase in a variety of ways, such as angrily, sarcastically or joyfully. Ask children to identify the feeling expressed.

➤ 3. Ask the class, "Have you ever looked like the person in this picture? How can people tell when you are happy, sad or frustrated even when you don't say a word?"

Remind children to listen for putdowns.

Grade 1 • **skill** 1

ACTIVITY 8

Name the Feeling

 Time Needed: 15 minutes

 Purpose: Through role-plays, students will identify and name feelings.

Main Ideas: People react differently to the same situation. Feelings affect behavior.

Materials: None

Using This Activity

1. Bring the class together in a circle, and ask for volunteers to do some acting. Most of these scenarios require only one student, but if any children are reluctant to act alone, they may do the role-plays in pairs or with you.

2. Instruct the "audience" to watch for the feeling(s) being portrayed and to pay particular attention to nonverbal communication, such as facial expression, body language and tone of voice. They should also watch and listen for putdowns. Ask the actor what feeling he or she was demonstrating.

3. Explain to the class that feelings affect how people behave. You might say that when they feel happy, they get along with other people. If they are angry at one friend, though, they might take it out on lots of other people too. If they are happy, they may not get upset about a small problem or disappointment. If they are already angry, sad or grumpy, little problems or disappointments seem large. Ask children to give examples of this in their own lives.

Ask students to report on put-downs witnessed or used since yesterday's lesson. [See Day 2 note.]

Suggested scenarios
• Someone calls you a bad name.
• Nobody will play with you at recess.
• Another child just pushed you down.
• You just had a nightmare.
• You are leaving for a trip to Disneyland tomorrow.
• Your teacher just praised your work.
• You lost the game you were playing with a friend.
• Your friend told you he/she did not want to be your best friend anymore.
• Your friend received a new toy that you have been wanting.
• Your older sister or brother won't let you watch your favorite television show.
• Your bike has a flat tire.
• Your lunch money is missing.
• You won first place in a race.
• You are going to the dentist.
• You hear thunder.

You may want to use some of these scenarios for creating a "Think About Why" skit as your Day 10 wrap-up project to share with the rest of the school.

Ask students to listen and watch for putdowns again.

Grade 1 • **skill** 1

Manners Matter

Ask children to report on put-downs they have witnessed, used or received since yesterday's lesson. [See Day 2 note.]

 Time Needed: 15-30 minutes depending upon whether guests are invited

Purpose: Students will review age-appropriate manners and contrast them with putdowns.

Main Idea: When we use putdowns, we are not being polite.

Materials: None

You may want to begin with a simple definition of manners as rules about how to behave around other people.

The class could be divided into small groups to discuss this question about the need for good manners. The students can then be brought together as a class to compare their answers.

Children may answer that manners are important because they help people work together, keep people from getting hurt emotionally or physically, make the school a safer place.

You may want to think about creating a chart that contrasts putdown responses and polite responses to use as your Day 10 wrap-up project to share with the rest of the school.

Using This Activity

1. Review any classroom behavior rules you have established, such as raising one's hand to speak, not talking when someone else is talking, not touching someone else's possessions without permission. Explain that these rules are examples of good manners. Adults and children try to follow good manners. Ask, "Why are good manners important in getting along with one another?"

2. Ask, "Why are we talking about manners in the same lesson as putdowns?" Help children understand that putdowns are the opposite of good manners because putdowns hurt people. When we use putdowns, we are not being polite.

3. Present several situations and ask children how to respond with manners instead of putdowns.

Situation	Putdown response	Polite response
•Somebody falls in a puddle	Laugh, call names	Help person get up
• Someone makes a mistake in class	Laugh, point finger	Let person try again
•Someone burps	Groan, mimic	Say nothing

4. If time allows, invite a cafeteria worker, bus driver, or other adult to class to explain manners in the context of their work with children.

Ask students to listen and watch for putdowns again.

Skill Wrap-up

 Time Needed: 10-15 minutes for review, longer for project

 Purpose: Students will review the main concepts of this skill.

 Main Ideas: Putdowns are words or actions that hurt another person.

Putdowns are often caused by strong feelings.

Materials: Varied, depending upon project

Using This Activity

1. Review the key concepts of this skill:

- Your feelings affect how you behave. If you are feeling upset, you are more likely to put someone down.

- Putdowns hurt people's feelings.

- You can tell how others feel by their facial expression and body language.

2. Help the class prepare a project that will take the message of "Think About Why" to the rest of the school. This can be done with posters, banners, newsletter, PA announcement, window decorations, poems or songs, or a class skit or video for a school assembly. Or, you might invite staff members or other adults to the class and allow your students to explain what they have learned.

Use this wrap-up on the tenth day of the skill, even if you have not had time to work through the entire skill.

Other classrooms in the school may also be creating projects for presentation to the rest of the school, so you may want to coordinate skill wrap-up efforts with other teachers or the administration.

At the end of this review, announce, "Next week we'll start a new skill called 'Stay Cool,' which teaches ways to stay calm when we are upset."

Please complete this brief evaluation at the conclusion of your work on this skill.

1. Activities in this skill which worked well for me were:

2. Activities in this skill which were meaningful to my class were:

3. Activities which needed adjustments were:

4. I was unable to complete the following lessons in the two week instructional period:

5. Ways in which I can include those lessons in my plans for the remainder of the year:

6. Ways to improve this unit for future *No Putdowns* work are:

GRADE 1

SKILL 2

Stay Cool

PUTDOWNS

A Program for Creating a Healthy
Learning Environment by Encouraging,
Understanding and Respecting

Getting angry is normal and healthy. But the way we express anger can lead to trouble. This can be a difficult concept for children — and some adults. Help children think about what they do when angry. Explain that it is okay to be angry, but it is not okay to express it by breaking things, hitting people, or using putdowns.

If *No Putdowns* was used in your school last year, treat this introduction as review. You might say, "You learned three strategies in kindergarten. Can you name them?" (The three are count to ten, take a deep breath, and telling yourself to "Freeze please." Students may also mention the strategy of whispering "Stay cool" to themselves.

If you are reviewing, ask students if they have used any of these "Stay Cool" strategies since they learned them in kindergarten.

Practice, along with instruction and reinforcement, are the keys to this skill. If a student is upset, treat the situation as a "teachable moment." Ask what strategy he or she could use. Point out when you notice a student staying cool. If a situation did get out of control, wait until things have settled down, then talk about what the participants could have done to stay cool. Focus on what can be improved, not what has gone wrong.

Introduction to Stay Cool

 Time Needed: 15 minutes

 Purpose: Students will be introduced to the concept of staying cool.

Main Idea: People can learn to manage their feelings.

 Materials: None

Using This Activity

➤ **1.** Bring the class together for a discussion and briefly review Skill 1, "Think About Why," in which the class learned about identifying feelings and how they can lead to certain behaviors.

2. Introduce "Stay Cool" by explaining that strong feelings, especially anger and fear, may be hard to handle. Sometimes we get so angry and upset we can't think clearly, and then we do things that aren't appropriate. For the next two weeks, the class will be talking about how to stay cool so they don't express their anger in harmful ways.

3. Ask students to tell about times when they felt as if they were out of control. What happened when they became very angry? How did their parents or friends react? Did the way they expressed their anger lead to more conflict?

4. Tell students that they can learn to manage or handle their feelings. They don't have to act out those angry feelings when they feel like exploding. They can learn to calm down and think about their actions.

Count to Ten

 Time Needed: 5 minutes

 Purpose: Students will recognize that there are strategies to use when troubled or angry.

 Main Idea: Counting to ten can help us calm down when we are angry.

 Materials: None

Using This Activity

1. Explain to the class that they are going to count to ten — on their fingers. Demonstrate two techniques: touch a finger to the fingers of the opposite hand as you count; and count one as you bend your thumb then touch the thumb to each of the fingers of the same hand to count from one to five, then repeat that pattern to count from six to ten.

2. Have the students count to ten using one of these tactile methods. Repeat several times.

3. Explain that some people will need to count to ten or more, while others become calmer at two or three. Ask students to predict how high they will have to count to calm down. Challenge them to become aware of their own stay cool needs: "Next time you are angry or upset, try counting. How high did you count before you felt calmer?"

Students learned the counting to ten strategy in kindergarten; however, this year, they use a tactile approach. The tactile element, as much as the counting, helps children calm down.

Describing Stay Cool

 Time Needed: 20 minutes

 Purpose: Students will understand the concept of staying cool.

 Main Idea: We can understand the feeling of staying cool by comparing it to physical sensations.

Materials: Chart paper and marker

Using This Activity

➤ **1.** Review the name of the skill, "Stay Cool," and ask the class what the phrase means.

➤ **2.** Review or introduce the five senses: seeing, hearing, tasting, touching and smelling.

3. Ask students to help you describe the feeling of staying cool by using their senses. Draw a line down the middle of the chart paper or board. On the lefthand side, you will be writing the senses and on the righthand side, student responses. Ask, "What does staying cool look (feel, taste, smell, sound) like?"

Staying Cool

Looks like...	
Smells like...	
Tastes like...	
Feels like...	
Sounds like...	

Staying cool simply means staying calm, taking a moment to think before acting. Be sure the class understands that staying cool does not mean never getting angry. It means knowing how to keep yourself in check even when angry.

Encourage the children to close their eyes and imagine "Stay Cool" with each sense and then tell you what came to mind: For example, it tastes like mint toothpaste, it smells like sunshine, or it looks like blue sky. You may want to explain that for "feels like", you are asking about a physical, not an emotional, quality. What does it feel like when you touch it? (For example, it feels like a soft flower.)

ACTIVITY 4

Take a Deep Breath

 Time Needed: 15 minutes

 Purpose: Students will learn to take a deep breath to stay cool.

Main Idea: Taking a deep breath can help you relax.

Materials: Plastic straws

Using This Activity

1. Demonstrate taking a slow, deep breath, then have the class try it several times.

2. Distribute straws. Instruct students to put the straws in their mouths and try to take a deep breath again. Ask, "How did that feel compared to breathing without the straw?"

3. Point out that breathing through the straw may have felt frustrating and made us tense. Compare feeling angry to breathing through a straw. When we are angry, breathing becomes more difficult and we become even more tense. That is why we must focus on taking deep breaths. Taking deep breaths can help us relax and calm down.

4. Have students take several slow, deep breaths without the straw to feel the difference.

Students may remember learning this "Stay Cool" strategy in kindergarten. If so, ask them to demonstrate it for you and to tell you how they have used it. Use this activity to help make the point that deep breathing is relaxing.

Watch for opportunities during the day to remind individual children to take deep breaths if they are getting upset. If the mood in the classroom is tense, stop for a "deep breath session" for the entire class.

Freeze Please

This is a good activity to do outside or during a physical education time.

Quick review of Red Light/Green Light
1. One student is "It," and turns away from the others who line up at a set point away from "It."
2. The child who is "It" calls "Green Light" and the other children move towards him or her. When "It" calls "Red Light," the other children must freeze. The child who is "It" turns around and tries to catch the other players moving. Any player caught moving after "Red Light" was called is out of the game.
3. The winner is the first person to tag the child who is "It."

If students learned this strategy in kindergarten, ask them to explain it to you instead! Then ask them to tell you how they have used it since they first learned it.

 Time Needed: 15 minutes

 Purpose: Students will learn to "freeze" when they are beginning to lose their cool.

 Main Idea: Freezing (or stopping) is a way to calm down

Materials: None

Using This Activity

➤ **1.** Allow students to play a game of "Red Light/Green Light" for a short time.

➤ **2.** After the game, gather the class in a circle to talk about the strategy of "Freeze Please" as a way to stay cool. Explain that the red light was like a time out, a time to STOP whatever they were doing. Green light allowed them to proceed again. "Freeze Please" is the same idea: Take a moment to STOP before taking action, especially before acting on an impulse to hit, shove, or use a putdown.

ACTIVITY 6

Hot and Cold

 Time Needed: 20 minutes

 Purpose: Students will be introduced to the association between heat and strong emotions such as anger.

Main Idea: When we feel angry (or hot), we need to cool down.

Materials: Chart paper and marker, or board and chalk

Using This Activity

1. Draw a line down the middle of the paper or board space, and label one side "Hot" and the other side "Cold."

2. Ask students to help you list things that are hot or warm. Write them in the "Hot" column.

   Students may name the stove, matches, lighters, heater, the sun, toaster, or even some foods, such as hot peppers or horseradish.

3. Ask students to help you list things that are cold or cool.

   Students may name ice cream, a freezer, snow, ice, a fan or air conditioner.

4. Ask, "What happens to you physically when you get angry, stressed or upset?" You are looking for answers such as, "I feel hot, my eyes burn, my hands get sweaty." Point out the similarities between hot things and what happens when people get angry.

   Students may need some help arriving at these symptoms. You may need to give some examples. All answers do not have to relate to the sensation of heat. Children may answer that their muscles get tight, or they have a (stomachache) or headache. Many children answer that they feel like hitting someone; however, that is what they want to do in response to their body feelings. In fact, wanting to punch or hit is a response to the tight muscles that need release.

5. Challenge students to keep themselves out of the "Hot" column! They want to stay cool. Point out that "Freeze Please" contains the word "freeze", which is a "cold" word.

6. End the activity with a chant, "Stay cool, Stay cool, Stay cool." Ask students to try to picture one of the items in the "Cold" column as they chant.

   Visualization of a cool or cold object is another way to stay cool!

Grade 1 • **skill** 2

Drawing Stay Cool

 Time Needed: Activity 7, 10 minutes for review, 20 minutes for picture and writing; Activity 8, 20 minutes

 Purpose: Students will review "Stay Cool" strategies.

Main Idea: We can choose a favorite "Stay Cool" strategy to practice in case we need it.

Materials: Drawing supplies

Using This Activity

Activity 7

1. Review the strategies and print them on the board as they are named: Count to ten, Take deep breaths, Say "Freeze please," Say "Stay cool."

2. Ask students to choose the strategy they think would work best for them and draw a picture of a situation in which they might use that strategy.

> **3.** After drawing the picture, have students label their drawings with the strategy they chose.

4. Challenge students to watch their own behavior overnight, and report back tomorrow about whether they used the strategy and how it worked.

Activity 8

> **5.** Ask students to do "show-and-tell" reports describing the situation in their drawings and the strategy selected. At this time, students can also report on their use of "Stay Cool" strategies since yesterday.

Students can tie the labeling into their writing process. Follow your usual writing procedure.

Urge students to continue to practice their "Stay Cool" strategies, even if their initial tries didn't feel very successful.

Grade 1 • **skill** 2

ACTIVITY 9

Who's Cool? Who's Not?

 Time Needed: 20 minutes

 Purpose: Students will identify fictional or historical characters who stayed cool or those who lost their cool.

Main Idea: Staying cool has important benefits; losing your cool can cause problems.

Materials: None

Using This Activity

1. Ask students to list book or movie characters or historical figures, and identify which ones stayed cool and which lost their cool.

2. Discuss what happened to those who stayed cool. Did they get what they wanted? Did they get hurt or hurt others? Did they help others? Did they earn respect?

3. Discuss what happened to those who did not stay cool. Did they get what they wanted? Did they get hurt or hurt others? Did they make matters better or worse?

4. Help students come to the conclusion that losing their cool can have negative consequences, while staying cool can help them think clearly, reduce the potential for harm, and achieve better results.

You may have to let the child tell the story to finally get to the consequences. Help children understand that the people who kept their cool usually got what they wanted or needed without hurting themselves or others. The people who lost their cool often lost more than just their cool! They hurt themselves or others or made the situation worse.

Ask children to think about fans, and bring in an actual fan or picture of a fan for class tomorrow. You may want to send a note home to parents to explain that you have asked children to bring in different kinds of fans as symbols of the skill they are completing. You are not asking them to bring in large box fans though! They can bring in personal fans, pictures, or make a fan at home to bring in.

 160

Skill Wrap-up

 Time Needed: 15 minutes

 Purpose: Students will use fans as a reminder to stay cool.

 Main Idea: The fan is a symbol of the "Stay Cool" skill because fans are used to cool us down.

 Materials: Fans or pictures of fans

Using This Activity

1. Allow students to display the fans or pictures they have brought in.

2. Discuss the purpose of fans (to stay cool!).

➤ **3.** Remind the class to think of the fan (or another cold object) when they need to stay cool.

Students may have chosen another cold object to visualize during the Day 6 activity and may continue to use that if they wish. Visualizing is effective as a "Stay Cool" strategy, but is even more effective if used while breathing deeply or counting to ten.

SKILL EVALUATION

Please complete this brief evaluation at the conclusion of your work on this skill.

1. Activities in this skill which worked well for me were:

2. Activities in this skill which were meaningful to my class were:

3. Activities which needed adjustments were:

4. I was unable to complete the following lessons in the two week instructional period:

5. Ways in which I can include those lessons in my plans for the remainder of the year:

6. Ways to improve this unit for future *No Putdowns* work are:

Shield Myself

A Program for Creating a Healthy Learning Environment by Encouraging, Understanding and Respecting

If your school used *No Putdowns* last year, treat this lesson as review. Ask students what they remember about this skill. In kindergarten, they spent several days creating "All About Me" booklets. They also learned that we all wear "I am special" signs which can be ripped apart by constant exposure to putdowns.

Use teachable moments to reinforce this skill. Discuss situations after participants have calmed down, and ask how they could have shielded themselves.

The kindergarten teachers may have used a large plastic hoop in "Shield Myself," as an image of the personal safety zone. It symbolizes our boundaries against putdowns. It is up to each of us to fill up the space inside that zone with positive thoughts and beliefs about ourselves as a defense against being hurt.

The umbrella keeps putdowns from drenching us.

Introduction to Shield Myself

 Time Needed: 15 minutes

 Purpose: Students will be introduced to "Shield Myself."

 Main Idea: We can protect ourselves from putdowns by recognizing our own strengths.

 Materials: None

Using This Activity

1. Review the first two skills: "Think About Why" and "Stay Cool."

2. Explain that for the next two weeks, the entire school will be studying Skill 3, "Shield Myself," which addresses self-esteem issues. A putdown does not change who we are inside. By feeling good about ourselves, we can keep putdowns from seriously hurting us.

➤ **3.** Call on a few students to name a positive trait about themselves, a talent or an accomplishment. Explain that we all need to be able to name things we like about ourselves — and we all have special strengths and talents. We need to recognize and appreciate them.

➤ **4.** Introduce the "Shield Myself" symbol of the umbrella. Ask what an umbrella does and why it is a good symbol for this skill.

I Am Special

 Time Needed: 30 minutes

 Purpose: Students will create personal signs as a reminder of their own specialness.

Main Idea: Each of us is special and deserves to be treated with respect.

Materials: Scissors, paper, crayons or markers, safety pins or ribbon

Using This Activity

1. Explain to the class that they will be making signs which can be worn around their necks or pinned to their clothing. The sign stands for their "self-concept" or how they feel about themselves. The sign is a reminder to the wearer and others that "I am special."

2. Distribute art materials and instruct students to cut the paper into a heart shape, circle, square, triangle or some other shape. Then have students illustrate or color the sign in a style of their choice.

3. Help students pin the sign to their clothing or put ribbon in it to wear as a necklace. Remind them that the sign means "I am special. I matter" and that belief is a shield against putdowns. Explain that when they look at another person's sign, it is a reminder to be respectful and kind, rather than rude or uncaring.

4. At the end of the day, talk about wearing the signs. Did another person's "I Am Special" sign stop them from putting that person down? Did their own signs shield them from putdowns or rude behavior?

Students may remember doing a similar activity in kindergarten when their class bear wore an "I Am Special" heart. In that activity, each putdown damaged the bear's sense of being special. His sign had been completely ripped apart by the end of the story. The next day, he was treated better and the sign was taped back together, but the putdowns did leave scars. Point out to the class that although the signs they are wearing can help shield them, too many putdowns can cause damage to one's self-esteem. But the stronger our sense of self-esteem, the harder it is to rip up our signs.

Some children are quite sure of their own importance and have a very healthy self-concept. This lesson is a good opportunity for them to realize that the people around them need to feel good about themselves too.

Class Chant

Self-talk is the inner voice that is constantly chattering at us. Many of us hear nothing but negative messages — putdowns — from that voice — "I can't do it, I failed again, everyone else is better than me, I'll probably strike out." That negative self-talk can become automatic, like a tape recording that just keeps playing. Negative self-talk holds us back, feeds our self-doubt and fears. Positive self-talk, however, is like having an internal cheering squad. If we learn to give ourselves positive messages, we feel more confident and successful. With practice, positive self-talk can replace self-putdowns. Positive self-talk also helps shield us from others. This lesson is an introduction to the power of positive messages. Tomorrow's activity will also deal with the energy that positive self-talk can generate.

A word of caution:
This skill addresses the importance of recognizing one's strengths and uniqueness, but it is not promoting boasting or puffing children up for false accomplishments.

As an optional step in this activity, have students try chanting negative statements: I am not happy. I can't learn new things. I am not a good kid. Talk about how those statements made children feel. Did they feel more energy when they chanted positive statements or negative statements? Help children understand that positive self-talk helps us feel good about ourselves and gives us energy and desire to do things. A steady diet of putdowns can really take the wind out of our sails!

Extending the Activity
Create your own class chant. Use it often. Encourage positive self-talk.

 Time Needed: 10-15 minutes

 Purpose: Students will learn about self-talk.

 Main Idea: The messages we say to ourselves influence how we feel and act.

 Materials: None

Using This Activity

1. Select students to take turns leading the class in positive self-talk chants. The leader will say the sentence once or twice, and then the class will repeat it.

   Possible chants:

   - I am happy.
   - I am caring.
   - I can learn new things.
   - I am a good kid!

2. Talk to students about the power of self-talk. How we talk to ourselves makes a big difference in how we feel about ourselves and other people. Positive self-talk shields us from hurtful words or actions. It can also help us strengthen our self-confidence.

The Little Engine Could and So Can You

 Time Needed: 20 minutes

 Purpose: Students will learn about self-talk through example.

Main Idea: Positive self-talk helped the Little Engine accom-plish a huge task.

Materials: *The Little Engine That Could* by Watty Piper

Using This Activity

1. Read or tell the story of *The Little Engine That Could.*

2. Discuss these questions:

How did the little engine talk to itself? What did it say?

What did the other engines say to it?

To whom did the little engine listen?

Did the little engine's "chant" and confidence help it accomplish its task?

Do you think the little engine was bragging when it said, "I think I can" and "I knew I could?"

What might have happened if the little engine had chanted, "I don't think I can"?

3. Ask students how the example of the Little Engine could help them meet a challenge. ◄

Athletes use visualization in training and competition to see themselves performing success-fully. Their visualization is a sophisticated version of "I think I can, I know I can!"

Extending the Activity
• Have students act out the story of the Little Engine.
• Have the class help you write another story with the same theme, for example, a beaver building a new dam.
• Have someone lead the class in the chant "I think I can."

                    Grade 1 • **skill** 3

Personal Shield

The personal shield helps students think about their own strengths and what they need in order to feel safe and happy. Explain that the shield stands for their self-esteem; it is another version of the "I Am Special" sign. A healthy self-concept acts as a shield, keeping putdowns from getting through.

 Time Needed: 30 minutes

 Purpose: Students will identify positive elements in their lives.

Main Idea: We can shield ourselves by keeping positive things in mind.

Materials: Personal shield worksheet, crayons or markers, magazines, glue

Using This Activity

1. The shield is divided into four parts. In the appropriate space, students will draw or paste pictures of:

    *   something they do well

    *   something they like

    *   something that makes them happy

    *   something that makes them feel safe

2. Review the concept of "Shield Myself" and discuss how students can use their personal shields to help them deal with putdowns and arguments.

My Personal Shield

I Do This Well	I Like to Do This
This Makes Me Happy	This Makes Me Feel Safe

Name_____

I Like Myself Because...

 Time Needed: 10-15 minutes

 Purpose: Students will identify something they like about themselves.

Main Idea: It is important to like ourselves.

 Materials: Paper, pencils

Using This Activity

1. Have students get some writing practice and learn about "Shield Myself" by completing this sentence:

I like myself today because....

2. Post their sentences on a bulletin board so that other students can read them during the day. Or include their writing practice in their journals or portfolios.

This is a sentence starter you could ask students to complete for themselves every few days (either in writing, orally or to themselves.)

You might also read some of them to the class at the end of the day, and then ask if anyone wants to say any other reasons for liking themselves today.

I Am Proud

Time Needed: 20 minutes

Purpose: Students will focus on something that makes them feel proud of themselves.

Main Idea: Take time to recognize your accomplishments and strengths.

Materials: "I Am Proud" buttons, safety pins

Teacher Preparation

Copy and cut out enough "I Am Proud" buttons for you and the entire class.

Using This Activity

1. Tell students something you are proud of today. Put on an "I Am Proud" button. Ask each student to tell you something he or she is proud of today, and then award a button.

Any accomplishment of which the child is proud should be related to an action he or she completed or performed. It doesn't have to be a big accomplishment, but it should not be related to owning something, unless the child earned it. For example, "I am proud that I earned money to buy myself a toy," not "I am proud of my new toy." Be sure children are specific about an accomplishment or ability. Don't accept as an answer, "I am the best ballplayer on my team." Ask why the child thinks that. Help pinpoint the source of the student's pride: "I stopped every ground ball that came to me."

Students can wear the button all day and at the end of the day go home and tell their families about the button. They also may be asked about the buttons in school and can tell about their special accomplishment or talent.

ACTIVITY 8

Oops! I Made a Mistake

Time Needed: 10 minutes

Purpose: Students will begin to learn about dealing with mistakes.

Main Idea: Everyone makes mistakes, but we can't let them ruin our day.

Materials: See Teacher Preparation below.

Teacher Preparation

Make an item that is obviously defective — a kite without a string, a photograph that is lopsided, a cake that has fallen.

Using This Activity

1. Show great excitement and pride as you display your creation to the class. Ask what they think of it.

2. After taking some responses, note that you knew there was a mistake and you did it on purpose — this time. Ask, "What if I hadn't realized I had made a mistake and you teased me? How could I handle it? What could I say to myself?"

3. Point out to the class that making a mistake doesn't mean we have to feel stupid all day long — and it doesn't take away from who we are. We can try hard not to make mistakes but accept them when they do happen. In fact, mistakes are an opportunity to learn. Sometimes we learn more from mistakes than successes!

◄ You can begin to tie in the concept of "Build Up" (Skill 5) with this activity also. Discuss what we can say to people when they do make mistakes, so that we don't put them down. One way is to focus on the positive points. For example, a funny-looking cake might still taste good. Another way is to acknowledge the mistake and the person's feeling: "I know you missed the ball and feel embarrassed."

This activity may be somewhat sophisticated for first-graders. However, the concept can be introduced without being over-whelming. Adjust this activity to the needs of your class.

Making Friends with Me

 Time Needed: 10 minutes

 Purpose: Students will review the kind ways their friends treat them and discuss how to be a good friend to themselves.

Main Idea: Be a good friend to yourself.

 Materials: Chart paper and marker, or chalkboard space

Using This Activity

1. Ask the class to help you make a list of the qualities that make someone a good friend. Why do you like the people who are your friends? How do they treat you? How do you treat them? Write the students' responses on the board.

2. Ask, "What would you do if someone put your friend down?"

3. Ask the class, "Are you as good a friend to yourself as you are to others? How can you be a good friend to yourself? What can you say to yourself when you make a mistake or are disappointed in yourself?"

ACTIVITY 10

Skill Wrap-up

 Time Needed: 15 -25 minutes

 Purpose: Students will review key skill concepts.

 Main Idea: Everyone hears putdowns, but there are ways to keep them from being too harmful.

 Materials: Art supplies

Using This Activity

1. Ask children to name ways they can keep putdowns from crushing their feelings.

2. Go around the room and ask the students to name what they like best about themselves.

3. Instruct children to draw pictures about the skill and to use the umbrella symbol in their pictures.

Please complete this brief evaluation at the conclusion of your work on this skill.

1. Activities in this skill which worked well for me were:

2. Activities in this skill which were meaningful to my class were:

3. Activities which needed adjustments were:

4. I was unable to complete the following lessons in the two week instructional period:

5. Ways in which I can include those lessons in my plans for the remainder of the year:

6. Ways to improve this unit for future *No Putdowns* work are:

SKILL 4

Choose a
Response

**A Program for Creating a Healthy
Learning Environment by Encouraging,
Understanding and Respecting**

Introduction to Choose a Response

Time Needed: 15 minutes

Purpose: Students will identify choices they can make when put down.

Main Idea: We have choices about how to deal with putdowns and strong feelings.

Materials: Chart paper or chalkboard space

Using This Activity

➤ **1.** Explain to the class that for the next two weeks they will be looking at ways they can respond to putdowns and other conflicts. Staying cool is one the class has learned. That helps keep them from "flying off the handle." It buys time to think clearly about what to do next — what action to choose. This skill presents some of the choices that are available.

➤ **2.** Present a putdown or conflict situation that you have witnessed at school, and ask children to brainstorm responses. Accept all responses without judgment, and write them on the board. Right now, the main point is that in any situation we have choices.

3. Point out that although we have a wide range of choices in everything we do, we toss out many of them based on rules, knowledge and experience. Briefly discuss the wisdom and consequences of each of the listed responses.

"Choose a Response" builds on Skill 2, "Stay Cool." What can you do instead of using a put-down? Many children and adults think they are at the mercy of their feelings. They "automatically" use a putdown, make wisecracks, yell or even hit. Others say nothing at all and let the hurt eat away at them. "Choose a Response" is designed to help children see that they have many choices about how to respond to a difficult situation.

Possible situations:
An older child is bothering you at the bus stop.
Someone pushes you down at recess.
You spilled your juice on yourself at lunch.
A classmate put down your best friend or sibling.

Students will probably give some responses which make you feel uncomfortable, such as physical retaliation, name-calling or tattling. But these are choices, even if they are not the choices you would encourage. Through a discussion of consequences, try to guide children to the understanding that some choices are more productive than others.

ACTIVITY 2

Stop!

 Time Needed: 20 minutes

 Purpose: Students will learn that telling people to "Stop" is an option when faced with a putdown or conflict.

Main Idea: We can ask someone to "Stop" if we don't like how they are treating us.

Materials: STOP signs, scissors, crayons or markers

Using This Activity

1. Distribute blank STOP signs to the class. Instruct children to print STOP on the signs, color them, and cut them out.

2. Explain that one way to respond to a putdown or angry situation is "Tell them to stop" by saying, "I don't like what you're saying and I want you to stop talking to me like that" or "That hurts my feelings and I don't want you to say (do) that anymore."

3. Allow children time to practice different ways to say stop. Discuss the importance of how they say it. Saying it in a whining or pleading voice may escalate the teasing. Saying stop in a calm tone of voice is more effective. Urge all children to understand that stop means stop. When someone says stop, it is important to listen and respond appropriately. It is also important to not say stop unless you mean it.

You may want to point out that telling someone to stop doesn't always work, or it may be one step in dealing with a conflict. If this strategy doesn't work, the child may have to try the next steps: Walk away or Tell an Adult.

Reinforce the use of this skill whenever possible: "I just heard so-and-so ask you to stop. Why are you still doing it?"

STOP SIGN

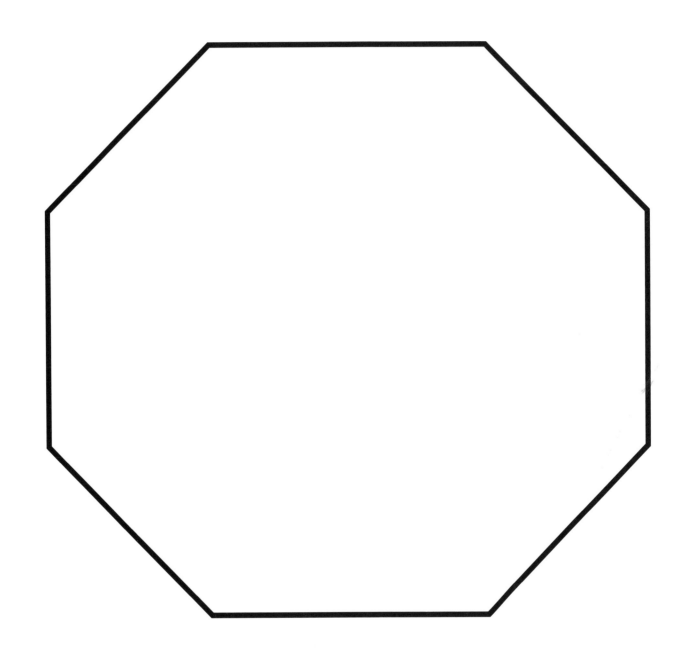

Walk Away

 Time Needed: 30 minutes

 Purpose: Students will learn that walking away is a choice to make when faced with a putdown or conflict

Main Idea: Sometimes, but not always, it is appropriate to walk away.

Materials: Crayons or markers, drawing paper

Using This Activity

1. Explain that sometimes "Tell them to stop" doesn't work and a child will have to try another plan, such as "Walk away." Some people think they can't walk away because that means they have "lost." But sometimes it is better to leave things alone rather than get into a fight.

2. Have students draw pictures to illustrate situations when it might be best to walk away.

3. Allow time for students to explain their pictures to the class.

This strategy is related to the idea of "choosing your battles." Sometimes it is necessary to deal with a situation, but sometimes it is best to leave it alone and walk away. "Walk away" may mean leaving the scene or it may mean "ignore it." Ignoring it is not the same as running away, though.

Throughout this skill, emphasize that we always have choices. This skill presents three positive, productive choices: Tell them to stop, Walk away, and Tell an adult.

Tell an Adult

Reasons for telling an adult:
I can't fix it myself.
An adult can help me.
Kids listen to adults.
I am in danger.

Students may also give some "inappropriate" reasons, such as "It will get so-and-so into trouble." This leads into the difference between telling for legitimate reasons and tattling. Tattling is defined here as telling for the sole purpose of getting the other person in trouble.

Make the point that often, "telling them to stop" or "walking away" will work. In most cases, the child should try those responses before telling an adult. But stress that you and other adults are there for them when they need help.

Children's expectations from an adult:
The adult can help solve the problem.
The adult can make it all better.
He or she can keep me from getting hurt.
Children may also say that the adult will punish the other child. Remind the class about the difference between telling an adult and tattling.
Point out that an adult may not fix the problem but may help a child figure out what to do.

 Time Needed: 20 minutes

 Purpose: Students will learn that they can go to an adult for help in a confrontation.

Main Idea: Sometimes a child needs adult help in handling a situation.

 Materials: Paper and pencil

Using This Activity

1. Discuss these questions:

- Why would you want to tell an adult about a conflict situation?

- What is the difference between tattling and telling an adult about a problem situation?

- What do you expect the adult to do for you?

2. Ask each child to choose an adult to whom he or she could talk. Then instruct each child to copy this sentence and fill in the name of that trusted adult:

3. I can talk to _____ about a problem.

Have children tape those slips of paper inside their desks or carry them in their backpacks as a reminder that telling an adult is an option.

ACTIVITY 5

Finding Your Way

 Time Needed: 20 minutes

 Purpose: Students will find the three strategies they have learned in "Choose a Response."

Main Idea: We have learned three responses to putdowns or conflicts.

Materials: Copies of maze

Using This Activity

Distribute the maze. Instruct the class to find the three "Choose a Response" strategies hidden in the maze.

Find the three ways to respond to a putdown.

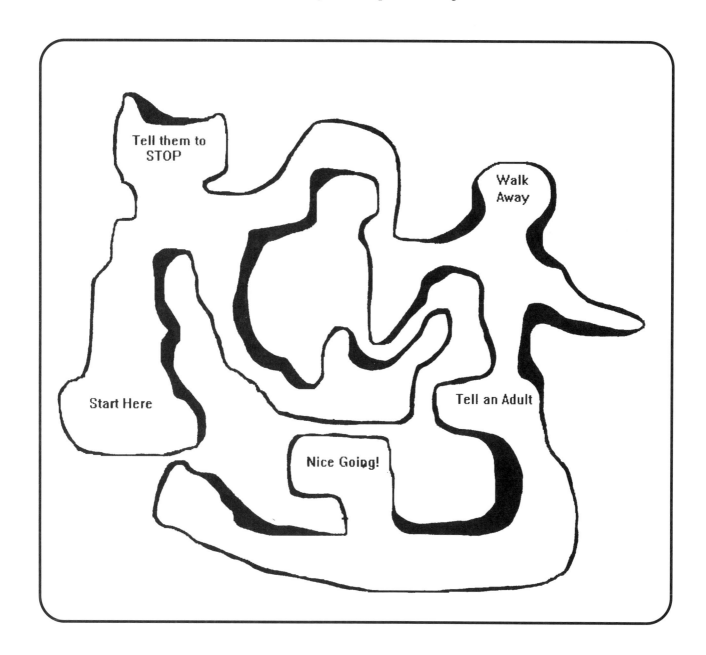

What Ugly Duckling?

 Time Needed: 15-20 minutes

 Purpose: Students will identify putdowns and responses.

 Main Idea: The Ugly Duckling was put down and made choices about how to respond.

 Materials: *The Ugly Duckling* by Hans Christian Andersen

Using This Activity

1. Read or tell the story *The Ugly Duckling*.

2. Ask the class to identify the putdowns in the story.

3. Ask how the Ugly Duckling responded to putdowns. What were the good and bad consequences of his responses?

4. Ask students how the story might have turned out if the little bird had chosen to respond differently?

◄ Ask about specific responses, for example, "What would have happened if the little duckling had put down the other animals? What would have happened if the little duckling had talked to a trusted adult?"

Extension Activity
A song about the Ugly Duckling was written by Frank Loesser for the Danny Kaye film *Hans Christian Andersen* (available on videotape). Show this segment of the film or teach the song to your class.

Responding with a Poem

 Time Needed: 15 minutes

 Purpose: Students will learn a poem to remind them they have choices.

 Main Idea: When conflict occurs, there are effective ways to deal with it.

Materials: None

Using This Activity

This poem can be practiced over several days. It can also be prepared for presentation with children clapping time and tapping their feet.

> **1.** Teach this poem to the class:

Conflict's okay, but don't let it cause trouble

You don't want to burst anyone's bubble.

We all get angry — don't you see?

Get your anger out, but don't hurt me.

Talking, waiting, walking away

Helps us all have a better day.

2. Ask children what conflict means. Use the simple definition that conflict is a disagreement between two or more people.

Sharing Time

 Time Needed: 20 minutes

 Purpose: Students will identify times when they witnessed or were involved in a conflict.

Main Idea: Looking at past situations can help us plan what to do next time.

Materials: Slips of paper with sentence starters and topics printed on them

Teacher Preparation

Write these sentence starters and topics on slips of paper:

• A conflict I saw

• I got into a conflict when . . .

• A time I almost got into a fight

• I was blamed when . . .

• A time I blamed someone

• I got angry when . . .

Put these slips of paper in a bowl or container.

Using This Activity

1. Have the class sit in a circle. Review class rules for discussion: listening, one person speaking at a time, etc.

2. Ask for a volunteer to draw a slip of paper from the bowl and read the topic or sentence starter aloud. That student will tell about an experience she or he had. Help the student by asking questions: What started it? Could it have been stopped? Did anyone get hurt? Did anyone yell? What were the short-term consequences? What were the long-term consequences?

3. Continue to ask for volunteers as time permits.

Make up your own sentence starters and topics too.

Allow children to tell their stories, but help them focus on what happened and what they could do differently next time.

The Bad Guys

Villains are usually presented as self-serving: They want their own way and will do whatever is necessary to get it! They often choose fighting and putdowns. It often seems as if the bad guys temporarily get their way but eventually lose in a big way! "The good guys" often end up fighting too, but ask if there might be a better way to respond.

If the stories your class chooses are heavy on violence, even in cartoons, you may want to talk about some of the consequences of violence in real life. Television rarely shows the pain or further ramifications of fighting. Ask children what would happen if someone really did get kicked.

You may want to point out that villains are often presented as totally bad and that is rarely the case about anyone. Everyone, even the people who hurt us, has feelings.

 Time Needed: 20 minutes

 Purpose: Students will identify fictional heroes and villains and talk about their choices.

Main Idea: Heroes and villains make choices about their behavior.

Materials: Chart paper or board space

Using This Activity

1. Make two columns on the board or chart paper. Ask the class to name "good guys" and "bad guys" from movies, television or books.

2. Ask if the villains have anything in common with one another. Do they try to avoid or reduce conflict? Do they use any of the "Choose a Response" strategies?

3. What do the good guys have in common? Do they try to avoid or reduce conflict?

Skill Wrap-up

This is an opportunity for the class to work together, an appropriate prelude to the final skill, "Build Up," which addresses the idea of community and being encouraging. Note how the class works on this project together so that you can refer to it next week when you introduce "Build Up."

 Time Needed: 30 minutes

 Purpose: Students will create a mural illustrating the choices they have learned.

 **Main Idea:** We have learned three responses to conflict: tell them to stop, walk away, tell an adult.

 Materials: Butcher paper, markers or crayons, photos or self-portraits

Using This Activity

1. Tape a four- or five-foot section of paper to the wall.

2. Help the class print on the paper:

```
Ms/Mr _____'s class can




Tell Them to Stop    Walk Away    Tell an Adult
```

3. Have groups of children take turns drawing pictures on the paper to create a mural. They can draw self-portraits, pictures of each strategy, or even post photos of themselves on the mural.

Please complete this brief evaluation at the conclusion of your work on this skill.

1. Activities in this skill which worked well for me were:

2. Activities in this skill which were meaningful to my class were:

3. Activities which needed adjustments were:

4. I was unable to complete the following lessons in the two week instructional period:

5. Ways in which I can include those lessons in my plans for the remainder of the year:

6. Ways to improve this unit for future *No Putdowns* work are:

GRADE
1

SKILL 5

Build Up

**A Program for Creating a Healthy
Learning Environment by Encouraging,
Understanding and Respecting**

Introduction to Build Up

 Time Needed: 10 minutes

 Purpose: Students will review previous *No Putdown* skills and be introduced to the final skill, "Build Up."

 Main Idea: Build up is the opposite of put down.

 Materials: None

Using This Activity

1. Explain to the class that for the next ten days, they are going to get plenty of practice learning to be good to themselves and each other.

2. Review the previous four skills:

Think About Why

Stay Cool

Shield Myself

Choose a Response

3. Explain that "Build Up" teaches what to do in place of putdowns. Building up is the opposite of putting down.

If most of your students participated in *No Putdowns* last year as kindergartners, treat this lesson as review. Ask students to tell you what they remember about "Build Up."

This last skill transfers *No Putdowns* from a school subject to practice on a daily basis. Up to this point, children have learned academically to recognize and handle putdowns, but they need practice building up themselves and others and replacing putdowns with positive statements. For many children — and adults — it is much easier to put down than to build up. Review the possible reasons for putdowns — habit, modeled behavior, strong feelings. Many children do not know what to say in place of putdowns. Now they will have the opportunity to practice this important life skill.

Stress that build up does not mean giving empty compliments or simply saying the right words. You have to mean them! It is about learning to be kind, courteous and caring.

What Does Building Up Look Like?

 Time Needed: 15 minutes

 Purpose: Students will learn characteristics of building up.

 Main Idea: Building up can be expressed in many ways.

 Materials: Chart paper and marker

Using This Activity

1. At the top of the page, print "Building Up." Underneath, draw three columns and label them:

    Looks Like   Sounds Like   Feels Like

> ◄ Explain that "Feels like" is referring to physical touching, not emotions. How do people express build-ups by touching each other?

2. Ask the class to help you fill in the columns of this chart to describe how building up looks, sounds and feels:

Building Up

Looks Like	Sounds Like	Feels Like
Smiling	"Good job"	Pat on the back
Thumbs-up sign	Applause	High five

Heart Mate

 Time Needed: 10 minutes

 Purpose: Students will practice giving compliments

 Main Idea: It feels good to give and receive compliments.

 Materials: Construction paper hearts

Teacher Preparation

Make one paper heart for every two students. Cut the hearts in half, in a variety of ways, so that no two halves are alike.

Using This Activity

1. Place the heart halves in a bag or box and shake them up.

2. Ask each student to take half a heart from the bag.

3. Instruct the students to find the person who has the other half of his/her heart.

4. Tell students that when they find their "heart-mate," they are to pay that person a compliment.

Teachers involved with *No Putdowns* have found that learning to give build ups requires a great deal of practice and reinforcement. Giving compliments and encouragement may feel false and awkward to children at first, but it does become more natural with practice.

Alike or Different?

 Time Needed: 15 minutes

 Purpose: Students will identify similarities and differences among themselves.

Main Idea: People have many similarities and differences.

Materials: Magazines with photos of people of different ages, races, interests, feelings, and so on

Using This Activity

1. Hold up pictures from the magazines and ask students to say whether the person in the picture is "like me" or "different than me." Ask what makes the person alike or different.

2. Ask what makes children in the class alike or different from one another.

Young children tend to think concretely and in terms of themselves. They also may be very blunt in their answers. But don't avoid discussion of differences and diversity. Often, children's comments about differences may sound like stereotypes or prejudice, but they are also trying to understand their world and are looking for help in doing so. Acknowledge that there are important differences among people in eye color, skin color, height, weight, and so on, but differences don't make one person correct and one person wrong. They are just different. Also point out how much even seemingly different people have in common.

Outlining My Friend

 Time Needed: 30 minutes

 Purpose: Students will practice writing encouraging comments.

Main Idea: We can encourage and appreciate each other.

Materials: Roll of butcher paper, crayons

Using This Activity

1. Divide the class into pairs.

2. Have one student of each pair lie on the paper to be traced. Then switch so the other student's outline can be traced.

3. Tell students to write encouragers or compliments in their partner's outlines. You may need to help them with this. Suggest phrases such as "Way to go," "You can do it," "You're great," "You are strong."

4. Cut out forms and display in your classroom and/or hallway.

You may want to brainstorm a list of adjectives or encouraging phrases for students to use if they have trouble coming up with their own. However, urge children to write encouragers that have some heart to them or are specific to the other child, rather than empty phrases.

If time permits, children can write encouraging phrases in other classmates' outlines as well. Or you might use this as an ongoing project throughout the ten days of this skill.

ACTIVITY 6

Thank You

 Time Needed: 20-30 minutes

 Purpose: Students will write a thank-you note to school workers.

Main Idea: Saying "thank you for what you do" is a way to build up others.

Materials: Chart paper or chalkboard space, paper and pencils

Using This Activity

1. Ask students to think about a person or group of people who make the school a nice place to be — a teacher, janitor, bus driver, cafeteria staff, principal, or other staff. List the people and the reasons on the board.

2. Ask children to write a note of appreciation to someone listed on the board. They are thanking that person or group for the special work they do, such as cleaning up, driving the bus safely, keeping the hall neat, and so on.

3. Arrange to have the notes delivered to the appropriate people in the school.

Many of your students may remember that last year they took a walk around the school and noted people making the school a better place.

Thank-you notes may be regarded as a lost courtesy, but they are a wonderful way to build up. Rarely will a person mind being recognized or thanked!

Storybook Encouragers

When a behavior is observed in literature or other media, it is processed and perhaps incorporated into one's own behavior. By recognizing the positive traits and behaviors of popular or beloved fictional characters, children may adjust their own actions.

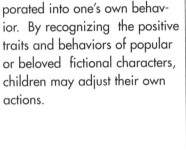

Time Needed: 10-15 minutes

Purpose: Students will identify characters who encourage others.

Main Idea: We can learn about encouragement in the stories we read or watch.

Materials: None

Using This Activity

1. Ask students to think about storybook characters who encouraged other characters. (For example, fairy godmothers are usually great encouragers.) What did they do to help or encourage others?

2. You might also want to extend this activity to include characters in movies, videos or other media.

ACTIVITY 8

Complete the Picture

 Time Needed: 20 minutes

 Purpose: Students will write an encouraging response for a difficult situation.

Main Idea: In a difficult or embarrassing situation, we can be supportive of others.

Materials: Copy of worksheet for each student

Using This Activity

1. Distribute worksheets. Explain that the little boy is very upset because he lost his favorite toy. Ask students to write (in the bubble) encouraging or build-up words that the little girl might say to him, for example, "Let me help you."

2. Ask students to share their responses with the rest of the class.

Extending the Activity

You might suggest other situations: What would you say to a friend who can't come out to play because he/she has a cold? What would you say to a friend who didn't get selected for a game?

Grade 1 • **skill** 5

Name_____

Circle Game

 Time Needed: 10 minutes

 Purpose: Students will encourage classmates.

 Main Idea: We can recognize positive traits in other people and provide encouragement.

 Materials: Beanbag or ball

Using This Activity

1. Sit in a circle with your students.

2. Toss the beanbag to a student and say something encouraging or complimentary to her or him.

3. Tell the recipient to toss the bag to someone else and say a compliment or encouraging word.

4. Continue tossing the beanbag around until everyone has had a turn to catch it and toss it to someone else along with an encouraging word.

◀ Urge your students to build up someone with whom they don't usually play. As a super challenge, ask them to build up someone with whom they don't usually get along!

No Putdowns Party

Although *No Putdowns* has been completed, continue throughout the year to make tie-ins whenever appropriate.

Students can present their "gift" statements to each other during the party.

A school-wide or even grade-level celebration will take planning by teachers and even parents since parents are part of the *No Putdowns* process. If parents are not included in the celebration, notify them that the formal instruction period of the program has ended, but the work is ongoing and constant both at home and at school.

Another choice is to have a "commencement" ceremony with presentation of the class certificates or other recognitions.

Time Needed: 30 minutes

Purpose: Students will celebrate the work they have done in ten weeks of *No Putdowns*.

Main Idea: This is the completion of the formal instruction period, but the skills take a lifetime of practice.

Materials: Depends upon activity chosen

Using This Activity

1. Have a party! The class has just completed ten weeks of *No Putdowns*. Today is a day to celebrate, have fun, and feel good about themselves and their classmates. Partying together is also an opportunity to build community and class goodwill.

2. Ask students to name a highlight of the program: something important that they learned.

3. If possible, have a grade-level or even school-wide celebration. That might mean treats in the cafeteria, a storyteller, games, a song person, etc.

Please complete this brief evaluation at the conclusion of your work on this skill.

1. Activities in this skill which worked well for me were:

2. Activities in this skill which were meaningful to my class were:

3. Activities which needed adjustments were:

4. I was unable to complete the following lessons in the two week instructional period:

5. Ways in which I can include those lessons in my plans for the remainder of the year:

6. Ways to improve this unit for future *No Putdowns* work are:

GRADE
2

**A Program for Creating a Healthy
Learning Environment by Encouraging,
Understanding and Respecting**

SOCIAL COMPETENCY TABLE
Grade 2

SOCIAL COMPETENCIES	NO PUTDOWNS SKILLS				
	Skill 1: Think About Why	**Skill 2:** Stay Cool	**Skill 3:** Shield Myself	**Skill 4:** Choose a Response	**Skill 5:** Build Up
Communication Skills	X	X	X	X	X
Empathy	X			X	X
Self-worth			X	X	X
Respect	X			X	X
Self-control		X		X	
Community Building			X	X	X
Conflict Resolution				X	
Anger/Stress Management		X	X	X	X
Problem-solving		X		X	X
Violence Prevention	X			X	

GRADE 2 ACTIVITIES

GRADE
2

SKILL 1

Think About Why

A Program for Creating a Healthy Learning Environment by Encouraging, Understanding and Respecting

Introduction to
No Putdowns

If most of your students participated in the *No Putdowns* program last year, treat this lesson as review rather than new information.

Time Needed: 15 minutes

Purpose: Students will be introduced to *No Putdowns* and Skill 1 "Think About Why."

Main Ideas: Entire school is participating in this program.

Putdowns are words or actions that hurt another person.

Putdowns are often caused by strong feelings.

Materials: None

Using This Activity

Putdowns are words or actions that are disrespectful to another person, place or thing. Putdowns are usually used for reasons of power, anger, fear, jealousy, habit, humor, frustration, or modeled behavior. See the teacher's manual for a full discussion of putdowns.

If this lesson is review, ask students if they can remember what the five *No Putdowns* skills are.

If the school is involved in other character education efforts, this is a good time to make the connection so that students see that *No Putdowns* is another piece of the puzzle of how to treat themselves and others.

1. Bring the class together for a discussion. Ask your class, "Has anyone ever hurt your feelings or said or done something that made you feel terrible?" [Students may talk about name-calling, pushing, spanking, scolding, being yelled at, being teased, and so on.]

➤ 2. Refer to the incidents of name-calling, being ignored or excluded, and teasing. Tell the class, "When someone makes fun of us or hurts our feelings, we call that a putdown."

➤ 3. Explain that "The entire school is starting a 10-week project called *No Putdowns*. The goals for the school and the class are to try not to use putdowns and to learn how to respond if someone does put you down."

4. Wrap up this introduction by asking, "Do you have any idea why you say mean things to your brothers or sisters or classmates sometimes?" [Children may answer that someone made them mad, they couldn't do something they wanted to do, or the other person had something they wanted.] Point out that they had strong feelings when they used the putdown, and strong feelings can cause people to react in many different ways. "For the next two weeks, we will do activities that help us identify putdowns and try to figure out some of the feelings that lead to putdowns. The name of the skill is 'Think About Why.'"

Identifying Putdowns

Time Needed: 15 minutes

Purpose: Students will learn to differentiate between putdowns and constructive criticism or discipline.

Main Idea: Putdowns are different than discipline or constructive criticism.

Materials: Index cards

Teacher Preparation:

On each index card, print an example of a putdown, constructive criticism, or disciplinary remark.

Using This Activity

1. Ask for volunteers to select index cards and read the comment aloud.

2. After each comment is read, ask the class if it is a putdown. Why or why not? Help students understand the differences between putdowns and more constructive comments.

This activity will be very effective if you use comments you have heard in your own school. Or use some of these comments:

"I want you to do your homework."

"Can't you ever do anything right?"

"Your new shirt is ugly."

"I like your other coat better."

"I don't want you to go out and play right now."

"You're not going out until you clean your room."

"Your room is a mess today."

"You are so messy."

"You really blew that spelling test."

"What do you think went wrong?"

"You're so stupid."

The issue of putdown vs. constructive criticism or discipline is often confusing. Sometimes students learning about putdowns cry, "Putdown!" any time a teacher or parent reprimands them or tells them what to do. Explore the differences between putdowns and other comments. You may also want to note that tone of voice can be a factor. For example, "Where did you get that shirt?" can be a compliment if said admiringly and a putdown if said in a sarcastic tone of voice.

Sharing Experiences

 Time Needed: 30 minutes

 Purpose: Students will explore the emotions behind putdowns.

 Main Idea: Many putdowns are the result of strong feelings.

Materials: Drawing paper, markers or crayons; or notebook paper and pencils

Using This Activity

1. Ask the class to help you list different kinds of putdowns. [Answers might include name-calling, finger-pointing, exclusion, making faces, rolling one's eyes, and sarcastic tone of voice.]

➤ 2. Ask students to draw or write about a time when they put someone down. Have them share that experience with the class or in a small group. Ask students to talk about why they used the putdown—what were they feeling at the time?

3. Ask students to draw or write about a time when they were the target of a putdown. Have them share the experiences with the class or in small groups. How did they feel when they were put down?

Students do not have to reveal names or embarrassing details about putting down or being put down. They should focus on their feelings, not the details of the situation.

Chain of Events

 Time Needed: Activity 4, 15 minutes; Activity 5, 30 minutes

 Purpose: Students will explore how one event triggers other events.

Main Ideas: Anger and hurt can lead to putdowns or hurting others.
A chain of events can be interrupted.

Materials: A chain-of-events story, such as: *A Fly Went By,* by Mike McClintock, *Buzz, Buzz, Buzz,* by Byron Barton, or *The Quarreling Book,* by Charlotte Zolotow

Using This Activity

Activity 4

1. Read the story to the class.

2. Discuss how one event led to another.

3. Reread part of the story. Ask for suggestions about how to interrupt the chain of events. What could a character have said or done differently?

Activity 5

1. Ask for five students to line up in front of the class.

2. Explain that they are going to make up a chain of events story about putdowns. You may want to get them started with a situation. For example, "Carlos' older brother told him he was stupid for thinking the big kids would let him play football with them. So, Carlos got mad and..." The first child will suggest how Carlos reacted. The next student will tell a negative consequence of that action, and so on. Remind the volunteers of yesterday's story to help them understand the instructions.

3. After the five students have completed their story, ask the class how the chain of putdowns could have been broken.

The object of this activity is to stress that putdowns, anger and hurt can spread like a forest fire. One "grump" can soon make everyone grumpy (or worse!).

You might introduce two ideas for stopping the chain:
Questioning: "Why did you do that?"
Statement: "Please stop doing that," or "I don't like it when you do that."
We will talk more about these strategies in Skill 4, "Choose a Response."

There are many possible responses. Allow students to use their imaginations to come up with ways to break the chain of putdowns. For example, you might suggest, "What if Carlos had simply asked two other children his own age to play?"

You can mention positive actions you have viewed and ask the class for more examples each day. If a particular child is commended, give him or her the strip of paper to add to the chain.

Point out to students that it will be especially fun to see if any of the positive actions broke a chain of putdowns.

4. Now explain, "We can also create a positive chain of events. Just as putdowns can spread, so can friendliness, cooperation and respect. During the next week, we will build a positive paper chain. At the end of each day, we'll take a few minutes to write on paper strips any positive things that happened throughout the day — compliments, helping others, cooperation, and so on. Let's see if one positive event can trigger others."

I Feel

 Time Needed: 15 minutes

 Purpose: Students will understand that feelings and actions are related.

Main Idea: Certain events cause us to have strong feelings.

Materials: Chart paper and marker

Using This Activity

1. Create a chart as shown

Things That Make Me...	
Sad	
Angry	
Scared	
Jealous	
Frustrated	
Embarrassed	

2. Ask the class to name situations or events that can lead to those feelings for them. Write their answers in the boxes on the right.

3. Discuss how the strong feelings listed on the left might make a child do something hurtful.

TV Time

 Time Needed: 10-15 minutes each activity

 Purpose: To explore the prevalence of putdowns on popular television shows and their impact on children's behavior.

 Main Idea: Putdowns are common on television shows and have an impact on our behavior.

Materials: TV Time Tally Sheet

Using This Activity

Activity 7

1. Review putdowns. Explain that there are a lot of putdowns on popular television shows. You may want to give examples that you have viewed. Often, viewers don't even notice the putdowns because they are so common and are so much a part of the humor on shows.

➤ 2. Instruct students to watch a half-hour sitcom tonight (one that is acceptable to their parents!) Distribute tally sheets. Students are to keep track of the number of putdowns they hear and to write down a few examples.

Activity 8

1. Ask students to report on the show they watched. How many putdowns did they record? Ask them to give examples.

2. Discuss why putdowns are so common on comedy shows. Why do audiences think putdowns are funny? Were the putdowns said in anger or for laughs — or both? How would students feel if someone made those comments to them?

Find out if any children are not allowed to watch television on school nights. If so, ask them to read a book and find examples of putdowns, or think about shows they have seen. Introduce the concept of using a putdown as humor. It is studied more thoroughly in later grades, but you can point out that sometimes we say putdowns and think we are being funny, but they still hurt the other person. Putdowns hurt real people even if they don't hurt on television. Script writers provide TV characters with their snappy comebacks. Real people often don't know what to say in response to putdowns.

You can use the information students gathered to make graphs, compute rankings, or add up the total number on the different shows viewed.

If students who watched the same show came up with very different putdown tallies, discuss the difference. For math practice, figure an average number of putdowns for that show.

Student Name_____

TV TIME TALLY SHEET

Show I Watched_____

That Was a Putdown!

Keep track of the number of putdowns you witness on this show by making checkmarks next to the numbers on the screen.

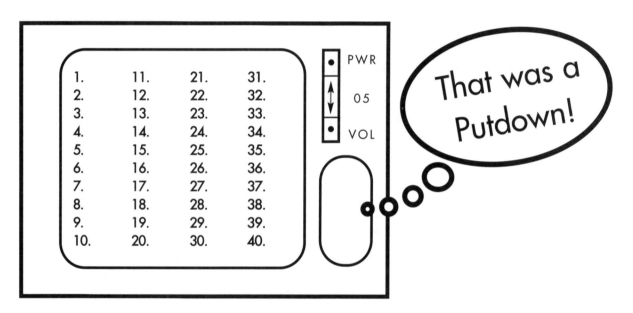

Look at These Putdowns!

Give two examples of putdowns that you heard or saw on the show.

1. _____

_____

2. _____

_____

Putdowns Chart

 Time Needed: 15 minutes

 Purpose: Students will explore the nature of putdowns.

 Main Idea: If putdowns can be imagined as tangible objects, we may have a better understanding of their impact.

 Materials: Chart paper and markers, or notepaper and pencils

Using This Activity

1. Copy this T-chart onto the board or chart paper.

	Putdowns
Feel like	
Look like	
Taste like	
Sound like	

2. Instruct students to complete the chart, either as a class, in small groups or individually. If done in small groups, distribute chart paper and marker to each group. Each group should select someone to copy the chart and record group answers. If done individually, instruct students to copy the chart onto notepaper.

3. Process student answers depending upon your choice of class, group or individual activity.

Remember, you are asking for physical characteristics. For example, for "feel like" you are asking for answers such as sandpaper or cactus, not emotions. Encourage students to use their senses and imaginations to fill in the chart.

Save the chart(s) that the class generated. The chart(s) or various images from the chart(s) could be presented tomorrow as a way of sharing understanding of this skill with the rest of the school. (See Day 10.)

Grade 2 • **skill** 1

Skill Wrap-up

 Time Needed: 10-15 minutes for review, longer for projects.

 Purpose: Students will review the main concepts in this skill.

Main Ideas: Strong feelings can lead to putdowns.

Putdowns are hurtful to other people.

Body language and facial expression can tell you how another person is feeling.

Putdowns are not the same as discipline or constructive criticism.

Materials: Varied, depending upon project space.

Using This Activity

1. Review the key concepts of Skill 1, "Think About Why."

2. Help the class prepare a project that will take the message of "Think About Why" to the rest of the school. You might decorate and display the charts created on Day 9. The class might create posters, banners, a newsletter, PA announcement, window decorations, poems or songs, class skit or video for a school assembly, or a logo for the skill. Or, you might invite staff members or other adults to the class and allow your students to explain what they learned.

Use this wrap-up on the last day of the skill, even if you have not had time to work through all the other activities in this skill.

Ask students if they witnessed or made any putdowns, and invite them to tell the class about them. Caution them not to use the names of other people involved.

Preview the next skill by announcing, "Next week we'll start a new skill called 'Stay Cool.' We'll learn more about how to stay calm when we are angry, frustrated or upset."

Please complete this brief evaluation at the conclusion of your work on this skill.

1. Activities in this skill which worked well for me were:

2. Activities in this skill which were meaningful to my class were:

3. Activities which needed adjustments were:

4. I was unable to complete the following lessons in the two week instructional period:

5. Ways in which I can include those lessons in my plans for the remainder of the year:

6. Ways to improve this unit for future *No Putdowns* work are:

GRADE
2

SKILL 2

Stay Cool

**A Program for Creating a Healthy
Learning Environment by Encouraging,
Understanding and Respecting**

Introduction to Stay Cool

 Time Needed: 15 minutes

 Purpose: Students will be introduced to "Stay Cool" skill.

 Main Idea: Sometimes anger is like a cup that gets so full it overflows.

 Materials: Cup, spoon, water

Using This Activity

➤ **1.** Briefly review Skill 1, "Think About Why," in which the class learned about identifying feelings and understanding that strong feelings can result in putdowns.

2. Explain that strong feelings, especially anger and fear, can be overwhelming. Sometimes we get so angry and upset we can't think clearly — and we express our feelings in harmful ways. For the next two weeks, the class will be talking about a new skill, "Stay Cool." It is all about learning to calm down.

➤ **3.** Show how feelings can become so overwhelming an "overflow" is inevitable. Add water to the cup a spoonful at a time. Each spoonful stands for a problem, difficult emotion, or something that causes stress. Keep adding water until it is filled to the very top. Ask, "What is going to happen if I add any more water to the cup?" When children answer it will overflow, add a few more spoonfuls to demonstrate.

4. Summarize the demonstration by explaining, "We can become filled to the brim with stress, and then it takes just one little thing to make us overflow. "Stay Cool" is about learning to calm down so that we don't get filled to the brim. Starting tomorrow, we will begin to learn the "Stay Cool' tricks that can help us take water out of the cup." [Remove some water with the spoon.]

Getting angry is normal and healthy, but the way we express anger can lead to trouble. This can be a difficult idea for children — and some adults. Help children think about what they do when angry. Explain that it is okay to be angry, but it is not okay to express it by breaking things, hitting people, or using putdowns.

You may want to start with some water in the cup. This makes it easier to fill the cup to the top and shows that we all have a certain degree or level of stress in our lives. That is, the cup will never be empty.

Countdown, but No Blast Off

 Time Needed: 10 minutes

 Purpose: Students will count down from ten to zero as a calming strategy.

 Main Ideas: Counting is a widely used "trick" to stay cool.

 Materials: None

Using This Activity

1. Ask students for suggestions about how to stay cool when they feel as if they are ready to "overflow." List the three "Stay Cool" strategies taught in earlier grades if students do not mention them: Take a deep breath, count to ten, Say to yourself, "Freeze, please" or "Stay cool." They may suggest taking a walk, thinking about something else, or hugging a pet or stuffed animal.

2. Focus especially on the counting strategy, pointing out that adults often use this to "buy some time" before speaking or doing. Although students may have learned this if they participated in *No Putdowns* in previous years, put a new twist on it this year. Now they will slowly count backwards from ten. (To make this even more effective, they can take a deep breath with each number.)

3. Remind students that these strategies work in many situations — when we are scared, getting ready to try something new, tense, or angry. These strategies are especially effective if we are on the verge of saying or doing something mean.

If the school is new to *No Putdowns*, spend extra time practicing deep breathing: counting to three as they inhale, holding for one, and counting to three as they exhale. Note that this relaxes the mind and the body.

Counting backwards may remind students of a space launch countdown, but here, the countdown is a cue not to blast off!

Practice, practice, and more practice along with instruction and reinforcement are the keys to "Stay Cool."
If a student is upset, treat the situation as a "teachable moment." Ask what strategy he or she could use. Point out when you notice a student staying cool. If a situation did get out of control, wait until things have settled down, then talk about what the participants could have done to stay cool. Focus on what can be improved, not what has gone wrong.

Mind Travel

 Time Needed: 15 minutes

 Purpose: Students will be introduced to visualization as a calming strategy.

Main Idea: We can relax by imagining a calm situation or scene.

Materials: None

Using This Activity

1. Introduce daydreaming. Students are probably familiar with these "trips" in which they seem to "go away" for a while without even realizing it. Explain, however, that in this activity, you are asking them to control their mind travel. If they are upset, they can choose to go away for a moment and then come right back. Ask, "Where could you go in your mind to calm down? It could be a place, a color, a pet, a sound, even a smell, something that is soothing and that you can picture vividly." Allow the class to try this technique.

2. Allow the class to try adding deep breathing to the technique. Breathing slowly and deeply while picturing something increases the effectiveness of this strategy.

3. Suggest that students decide ahead of time where they will go when they need to "get away" for a moment. But caution them that this technique is not the same as "spacing out" and ignoring someone who is talking to them. It is meant to be a very quick trip!

➤ 4. Discuss when this technique would be appropriate and when it wouldn't!

5. Have students try it with their eyes closed and again with eyes open. Allow only a second or two each time. They really can travel a long way and return calmer.

This strategy works especially well when a brother, sister or friend calls them a name. It is also effective when they feel left out, lonely or overwhelmed. It is not a good idea if an adult is talking to them or they are in danger.

Secret Signal

 Time Needed: 10 minutes

 Purpose: Students will devise personal signals to remind themselves to stay cool.

 Main Idea: We can remind ourselves to calm down by having our own secret signal.

 Materials: None

Using This Activity

1. Introduce the idea of a personal "secret signal." Students can use it whenever they are ready to lose their cool. They don't have to tell anyone else the signal. It is something they can do to remind themselves to stay cool.

2. Ask students for some suggestions (put a hand in a pocket, squeeze the thumb, fold hands). Then let students privately choose one of those signals or make up their own.

3. Remind students this is a private signal for their own use. When they feel themselves overflowing, they can give themselves the signal to stay cool.

Obviously, you do not want children to become dependent on a habit, but this does work when they are starting to lose control. Field tests of *No Putdowns* have shown this to be a very popular activity.

Other possible signals include: touch an elbow, hook index finger over thumb, spread fingers in a "stop" gesture, hold wrist with opposite hand.

Give It a Try!

 Time Needed: 25 minutes

 Purpose: Students will choose a "Stay Cool" strategy to try out for the next few days.

 Main Idea: We can choose a strategy in advance and choose to use it when we are upset.

Materials: Chart paper and markers

Teacher Preparation:

On chart paper, create bar graphs for each strategy as shown below. Each bar should have as many spaces as there are students. This can be set up either vertically or horizontally.

Count to ten

Take a deep breath

Use a secret signal

Take a quick mind trip

You may want to leave the bar graphs unlabeled and print in the strategies as students name them.

Using This Activity

1. Review the "Stay Cool" strategies.

2. Call upon students to come up one at a time and choose the strategy they are committed to using for the next two days when they feel overwhelmed. They can choose the one they like the best or the one they think would be easiest to remember to use.

3. Note the variety of choices and that different strategies work for different people.

Tension Barometer

 Time Needed: 30 minutes

 Purpose: Students will create personal tension barometers.

 Main Idea: Become aware of your tension level, and if it is rising, try to use your "Stay Cool" strategies.

 **Materials:** White paper (5 1/2" x 8 1/2"), strips of red paper (3 1/2" x 8 1/2"), tape, scissors

Teacher Preparation:

 Make a tension barometer for children to copy: Make slits in the white paper as indicated and slip the strip of red paper through the slits and over the white paper. On the paper, write the labels (from top to bottom): Ready to overflow, Very tense, Tense, Calm, Very calm.

Using This Activity

1. Distribute supplies to students and help them construct their own tension barometers.

2. Instruct students to tape their tension barometers to their desks or place inside a folder to protect it. Place yours on your desk or on a bulletin board so that it is visible to the class. Explain that throughout the day, they can adjust their barometers to reflect their feelings. You may want to ask during the next days, "How are you feeling? Adjust your tension barometers to let the rest of the class know."

This activity allows students to reflect on their own tension levels throughout the day. You may want to ask for a tension reading as you switch subjects during the day. By regularly tuning in, students can start to see what specifically makes them tense or relaxed in school.

If students start to feel their tension rising, it is time for them to use a "Stay Cool" strategy to keep themselves from reaching the overflow mark.

Remember to adjust your own tension barometer. Students can see that you have good days and bad days too. They may even begin to catch on to your need for more cooperation to reduce your tension level. This is a good opportunity to point out that we can help others stay cool by being sensitive to their tension levels.

Storybook Cool

 Time Needed: Activity 7, 20 minutes; Activity 8, 30 minutes

 Purpose: Students will identify characters who did and did not stay cool.

 Main Idea: Our favorite characters can help us learn about staying cool.

 Materials: Day 7, none; Day 8, art materials

Using This Activity

Activity 7

➤ **1.** Ask students to tell you about storybook or nursery rhyme characters who did not stay cool. What happened because they did not stay cool?

➤ **2.** Ask about characters from storybooks and nursery rhymes who did stay cool. What happened to them?

3. Discuss why it is important to stay cool in a difficult situation.

Activity 8

➤ **1.** Explain that students are to create posters about staying cool using characters they talked about yesterday. Students may work individually or in pairs.

2. Allow time for children to share their work or help hang it on the walls for display.

Characters who lost their cool include: Chicken Little, many Aesop characters, the troll in *Three Billy Goats Gruff*, the wolf in *The Three Little Pigs*.

Characters who kept their cool include: the third pig in *The Three Little Pigs*; the tortoise in "The Tortoise and the Hare", the animals in *Homeward Bound*.

The posters can be as simple as, "Little Red Riding Hood says 'Stay Cool'." The poster might feature a picture of Chicken Little saying, "The sky wasn't falling. I just lost my cool."

Send us copies of posters for possible use in the *No Putdowns* newsletter. Address mail to: *No Putdowns*, c/o CONTACT-Syracuse, P.O. Box 6149, Syracuse, New York 13217.

Stay Cool Role-plays

 Time Needed: 15 minutes

 Purpose: Students will practice "Stay Cool" strategies in role-plays.

Main Idea: Practicing appropriate responses helps make them easier to do in real situations.

Materials: None

Using This Activity

1. Have the class sit in a circle. Ask for volunteers, or call on children to role play situations with you or with each other. Present situations that are likely to make children lose their cool:

•Your little sister broke your favorite toy.

•Your mother punished you for something you didn't do.

•You can't find your shoes and the bus is waiting for you.

•You were supposed to spend the weekend with your father and he forgot.

2. The actors should respond to the situations as if they are beginning to lose their cool. "Freeze frame" situations as the tension rises. Ask: "How can you calm down? What technique would work best for you in this situation?"

You may want to have the child use the technique chosen on Day 5, when the bar charts were colored in.

This activity may be used at any time as a review or for practice and reinforcement.

Skill Wrap-up

 Time Needed: 25 minutes

 Purpose: Students will review concepts of "Stay Cool."

 Main Idea: We can train ourselves to stay cool.

 Materials: Chart paper and markers

Using This Activity

1. Review the strategies presented in this skill: Count to ten (backwards or forwards), deep breathing, take a short trip, and secret signal. Ask students what their favorite part of this skill was.

➤ 2. Do group writing by having the class work together to write a poem about staying cool. Remind them of the skill symbol — the fan — as something to work into the poem.

Tie into any writing you may be doing — haiku, limericks, choral reading, etc.

SKILL EVALUATION

Please complete this brief evaluation at the conclusion of your work on this skill.

1.   Activities in this skill which worked well for me were:

2.   Activities in this skill which were meaningful to my class were:

3.   Activities which needed adjustments were:

4.   I was unable to complete the following lessons in the two week instructional period:

5.   Ways in which I can include those lessons in my plans for the remainder of the year:

6.   Ways to improve this unit for future *No Putdowns* work are:

SKILL 3

Shield Myself

A Program for Creating a Healthy Learning Environment by Encouraging, Understanding and Respecting

Introduction to Shield Myself

 Time Needed: 15 minutes

Purpose: Students will be introduced to the "Shield Myself" skill.

Main Idea: We can protect ourselves from putdowns by recognizing our own strengths.

Materials: None

Using This Activity

1. Review the first two skills: "Think About Why" and "Stay Cool."

2. Explain that for the next two weeks, the entire school will be studying a new skill, "Shield Myself." This skill is about self-esteem, recognizing one's own strengths and forming a positive self-image. By feeling good about ourselves, we can keep putdowns from seriously hurting us. A putdown does not change who we are.

3. Call on a few students to name one positive trait about themselves — something they do well, an accomplishment, a talent. Explain that we all need to be able to name things we like about ourselves — and we all have a lot to be proud of. We all have special strengths and talents, and we need to discover them.

4. Ask students if they ever put themselves down. Do they ever call themselves "stupid" or "clumsy" or get down on themselves for making a mistake? Tell the class that "Shield Myself" also means learning to talk positively to ourselves instead of putting ourselves down.

5. Discuss the symbol for "Shield Myself" — an umbrella. Why is the umbrella a good symbol for this skill?

If your school used *No Putdowns* last year, treat this lesson as review. Ask students if they remember learning about this skill and what they did last year to help them feel good about themselves.

"Shield Myself" ties into many self-awareness, self-esteem activities with which you may be familiar. Feel free to substitute some of your favorite activities or relate "Shield Myself" to activities the class has done.

Use teachable moments to reinforce this skill. If situations arise, ask how students could have shielded themselves. Or discuss the situation that occurred, and ask what the participants could have done differently.

Some students may remember the image of the plastic hoop in previous "Shield Myself" discussions. The hoop serves as an image of the personal safety zone. It symbolizes our boundaries against putdowns. It is up to each of us to fill up the space inside that zone with positive thoughts and beliefs about ourselves as a defense against being hurt.

The umbrella keeps putdowns from drenching us. It is a shield against stormy weather.

ACTIVITY 2

I Feel Good

 Time Needed: 15 minutes

 Purpose: Students will learn why it is important to feel good about themselves.

Main Idea: We can protect ourselves from putdowns when we feel good about ourselves.

Materials: None

Using This Activity

1. Ask students to think of a time when they felt good about something they did for themselves or others. As children name these deeds, write them on the board:

   I hit a home run.

   I helped Mom wash the car.

   I shared my candy with my sister.

   I counted to ten instead of yelling.

   I made dinner myself.

   I told a good joke.

2. Explain that we can all do things that make us feel good about ourselves. They don't have to be huge accomplishments. Doing something for others, or doing well at an activity, builds self-confidence. We see that we are capable people. The better we feel about ourselves, the better we are able to shield ourselves from putdowns. When we feel worthless, it is easy for people to hurt us. When we feel good about ourselves, other people can't hurt us as easily because we have an invisible shield called self-worth.

◄ Children do not have to name huge accomplishments. In fact, the small, everyday accomplishments, courtesies and good deeds are a more effective teaching tool because children will see that they don't have to be superheroes or athletes to feel good about themselves. The thing they feel good about should be an action, though, and not an item they own (unless they feel good because they earned the money to buy the item, bought it as a gift, or helped pick it out for someone else). It can be as small as, "I brushed my teeth without being told." Encourage children to think reflectively and honestly before naming their accomplishments.

You may want to staple a note to children's bags to let parents know what this activity is all about:

Dear Parent,

I have asked your child to bring in items that tell about who he or she is. The items will be displayed for a short time tomorrow and then sent home again in this bag. This is part of the "Shield Myself" skill of our schoolwide *No Putdowns* program. Children learn to shield themselves from putdowns by developing self-confidence, recognizing their interests and talents, and knowing they are part of a family and a community.

Feel free to bring in a bag filled with things that let the class know more about who you are outside of school!

Part of knowing who we are is knowing we belong to a community. By helping to foster a sense of community in the classroom, children develop self-confidence and a closeness that results in fewer putdowns.

This Is My Bag

 Time Needed: Activity 3, 15-30 min.; Activity 4, 25-30 min.

 Purpose: Students will identify and display items which represent who they are.

Main Idea: We all have interests and strengths we can feel good about.

Materials: Paper bag for each student, art supplies, note to parents

Using This Activity

Activity 3

1. Distribute paper bags to the class. Explain that their homework is to collect in their bags items that show their interests, hobbies, beliefs and goals. They can also include items that tell about their families. The items can be photos, drawings, books, objects (shells, fossils, baseball, doll, etc.), and so on. They will be displaying the contents tomorrow.

2. During class time (or as homework) have students decorate their bags with "Shield Myself" messages or pictures that show their interests and favorite activities.

Activity 4

1. During the class *No Putdowns* time, instruct students to set up the contents of their bags as museum displays.

2. Allow students time to "tour the exhibits" and learn more about their classmates.

3. Bring the class back together and ask what they observed: Were there any similarities among the many exhibits? What did they find most interesting?

▶ **4.** Sum up the activity by pointing out that part of shielding ourselves is knowing about ourselves — what we like, what we like to do, what our strengths are. Another part of shielding ourselves is feeling as if we belong to a community. Did learning about their classmates help bring them together as a community?

I Am Proud

 Time Needed: Five minutes for each of next five days

 Purpose: Students will identify something which makes them feel proud of themselves on each of the next five days.

Main Idea: Every day we do something about which we can be proud.

Materials: "I Am Proud" chart

Using This Activity

1. Distribute blank charts to the class. Have students fill in today's date in the first box and then the dates for the next four days.

2. Explain that for each of the next five days, students are to write down something that made them feel proud that day. As in the Day 1 activity, the accomplishment does not have to be a huge one. Once again, remind students that feeling confident about themselves is a good way to shield themselves from putdowns and hurt feelings.

◄ Get the ball rolling by sharing something you are proud about today.

Students will use their completed calendars on Day 9.

At the end of the five days, collect the charts. Put a star or other sticker in the sixth box, or if you have time, write a comment. Ask students to share some of their accomplishments with the rest of the class. If this activity is begun on the sixth day, it will be completed on the tenth and last day of the skill. That is a perfect time to share accomplishments.

Name_____

If I Were an Animal

 Time Needed: 20-30 minutes

 Purpose: Students will identify with an animal based on traits and habits.

Main Idea: Learn to understand yourself better by thinking about what animal you would be.

Materials: Book and magazines featuring wide variety of animals

Using This Activity

1. Assign this writing activity to the class: What kind of animal would you be if you were animal? What traits, habits and special strengths do you admire or have in common with that animal?

◄ Stress that you are talking about traits, not appearance!

2. Tally on the board what animals students chose. Ask students who named the same or similar animals to talk about their choice. Do these students have a lot in common? Do they usually play or work together? Do they have similar interests or abilities? Is the class surprised at the choices of some of the students?

Remind the class to fill in their "I Am Proud" worksheets.

What Do You Do Well?

 Time Needed: 15 minutes

 Purpose: Students will recognize their own strengths and weaknesses.

 Main Idea: We all have strengths and weaknesses.

 Materials: None

Using This Activity

1. Ask the children to pull their chairs into a circle to discuss:

Who is good at art?

Who is good at sports?

Who has the best printing?

Who is a good singer?

Who is funny?

Who is a good speller?

2. Tell students something that you know you are good at and something you know you don't do very well. Ask students to name something they do well and something they wish they did better.

3. Discuss the importance of knowing what we do well and what we don't. Part of shielding oneself is recognizing one's weaknesses. If we can be realistic about our talents, others can't hurt our feelings as easily: "Hey, you sure don't know how to draw." "Yeah, I know I don't draw very well. But I am really good at arm wrestling and singing."

4. Ask children to talk about things they are working on improving. Have them complete this sentence: I would like to be better at _____, and I can work on improving by _____.

By this age, many students may be reluctant to talk about things they do well. They may be able to name their weaknesses more easily. Other students, however, may be prone to bragging and may need help talking about any weaknesses. It is important for students to be able to assess themselves realistically.

These "rebuttals" may take the form of self-talk rather than a verbal response to the putdown. Caution children to think about whether responding aloud is a good idea or whether it will fuel the situation. Maybe it is enough to say to oneself, "I have value, and I can do these other things well."

Point out that people have the power to change some things about themselves but not others! Remind them to focus on the things they can improve and not beat themselves up about the things they can't change.

Remind the class to fill in their "I Am Proud" worksheets.

Grade 2 • **skill** 3

Being a Friend to Yourself

 Time Needed: 15 minutes

 Purpose: Students will learn to encourage themselves.

 Main Idea: We should treat ourselves as well as we treat our best friends.

 Materials: None

Using This Activity

1. Ask the class, "What do you say to yourself when you make a mistake?" Write answers on the board, and don't make any comment or judgment about students' answers.

2. Point to various answers on the board and ask, "Would you say that to a friend?" Pay special attention to the self-deprecating comments. Ask, "If you wouldn't say that to a friend, why would you say that to yourself?"

3. Talk about being a good friend to yourself. Does a friend put a friend down? Then why would you put yourself down for making a mistake? Do you encourage your friends? Then why not encourage yourself?

Remind the class to fill in their "I Am Proud" worksheets.

Grade 2 • **skill** 3

I Am Proud Follow-up

 Time Needed: 20 minutes

 Purpose: Students will have an opportunity to share their "I Am Proud" experiences.

Main Idea: Telling other people what makes us proud helps them get to know us better.

 **Materials:** Completed "I Am Proud" worksheets, index cards

Using This Activity

1. Have students complete the last box of their "I Am Proud" worksheets.

2. Distribute index cards, and instruct students to write one "I Am Proud" statement from their completed worksheets. Instruct them to write their initials on the back.

3. Collect the cards, and arrange them on a desk or drop them into a box or bag.

4. Invite a student to come up and select a card and read the statement (The student should not select his or her own card). Allow that student an opportunity to guess whose card it is. If he or she does not guess correctly, ask for help from the class.

Caution students to write their names in small letters on the back of the index card or to use initials only.

This can be done over several days as a filler rather than in one session.

ACTIVITY 10

Skill Wrap-up

 Time Needed: 10 minutes

 Purpose: Students will review "Shield Myself" concepts.

 Main Idea: The ribbon is a reminder to shield myself when someone puts me down.

 Materials: Copies of ribbon

Using This Activity

1. Review the concepts of "Shield Myself." We can protect ourselves from putdowns and other hurts by feeling good about ourselves and by recognizing both our strengths and weaknesses. Remind students that we must stop putting ourselves down!

2. Distribute the ribbons as a reminder of these concepts.

Extending the Activity

Use stories or songs about characters who shielded themselves.

Suggested reading:

Silly Goose, Jack Kent
Amazing Grace, Mary Hoffman.

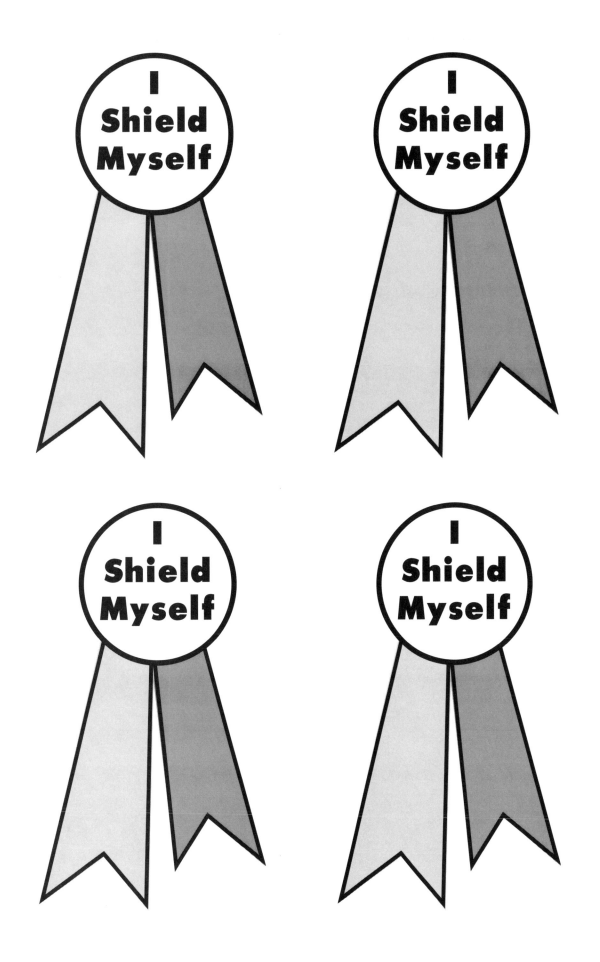

SKILL EVALUATION

Please complete this brief evaluation at the conclusion of your work on this skill.

1. Activities in this skill which worked well for me were:

2. Activities in this skill which were meaningful to my class were:

3. Activities which needed adjustments were:

4. I was unable to complete the following lessons in the two week instructional period:

5. Ways in which I can include those lessons in my plans for the remainder of the year:

6. Ways to improve this unit for future *No Putdowns* work are:

SKILL 4

Choose a
Response

NO PUTDOWNS

**A Program for Creating a Healthy
Learning Environment by Encouraging,
Understanding and Respecting**

Introduction to Choose a Response

 Time Needed: 10 minutes

 Purpose: Students will learn that they always have a choice about how to respond.

Main Idea: We always have choices, even in difficult situations.

Materials: Optional: Weather forecast from newspaper or video of weathercast

Using This Activity

1. Discuss the weather! Watch a tape of a weathercast, or bring in the weather page from your newspaper. Discuss the idea that we choose our clothing and even our activities based on the weather. If a hurricane is threatening, people make a choice: to leave or to stay and "weather the storm." People cannot change the weather, but they make choices about how to deal with it.

2. Direct discussion to choices children make based on the weather. Ask, "What do you do when it rains? What do you do to take care of yourself when it snows? How does the weather or the temperature affect the choices you make?"

3. Focus discussion on the idea of choices. We make choices all the time about how to respond. We cannot control the weather, but we can make ourselves more comfortable by dressing appropriately, choosing activities suitable for the weather, and even learning to adapt to the conditions. For the next two weeks, the class will focus on the choices they can make when confronted with a difficult situation. We cannot control other people, but we can control our attitudes, how we treat other people, and what we say.

ACTIVITY 2

"Hot Potato"

 Time Needed: 20 minutes

 Purpose: Students will identify commonly used responses.

 Main Idea: We choose how to respond to conflicts.

 Materials: Small ball, music

Using This Activity

1. Bring the class into a circle. Explain that they are going to play a game of "Hot Potato," with a new rule. Whoever is caught holding the "potato" when the music stops is out of the game, but he or she has to answer this question before sitting down: "What do you do or how do you act when you are angry or upset?"

2. Record answers on the board, for example, "Get angry, yell, get quiet, spend time by myself, hit back."

3. When the game is over, look at the list of responses. Some are safer than others, some keep conflict going, and some resolve the conflict. Some will work in some situations but not in others, but they are all choices. We decide which to use.

You may need to ask some leading questions to help students tell how they respond when upset. You might ask, "What do you do if your friend won't let you sit next to her? How do you act if you forget your sneakers on gym day? What do you do if your brother calls you a name?"

Make an analogy about the list of choices and a menu at a restaurant. Many choices are listed on the menu, and we have to choose what we want to eat. If we like the meal, we will probably order the same thing again; if we didn't like it, we will try something else next time. In a conflict, we try a response. If it works, we use it again; if it does not work, we need to try something else.

Eye to Eye

Time Needed: 15 minutes

Purpose: Students will recognize that making eye contact is a way to respond to a conflict.

Main Idea: Making eye contact can help you connect with another person.

Materials: None

Using This Activity

1. Pair up students for a staring contest. They will see who can stare longer in each pair and which pair can stare at each other the longest. Students may blink but are not to look away. When one person in each pair looks away, the other partner is the "winner," but they are out of the competition for the longest-staring pair.

2. Process the contest by explaining that making eye contact is a way to respond to a putdown or conflict. Instead of running away or looking away, a student can look the other person in the eye and make a personal connection. Making that connection can focus the other person's attention, defuse the situation, make the other person stop, or help two people connect emotionally.

Looking down may mean you are afraid, embarrassed or upset. Looking away or looking beyond the other person may mean that you do not think he or she is important, you are ignoring the other person, or you are not listening.

Some cultural issues are involved with this strategy. Eye contact is considered offensive in some cultures, so teachers may need to caution children to be sensitive to these differences. However, in the U.S. and other Western cultures, eye contact is considered part of good communication.

Remind students that making eye contact is different from staring (as they did in the contest). Staring at someone else can make him or her feel embarrassed or even angry. Making eye contact, however, can help people connect and see each other as individuals.

ACTIVITY 4

Ears to Hear

 Time Needed: 15 minutes

 Purpose: Students will practice listening and responding.

 Main Idea: We can choose to listen carefully.

 Materials: None

Using This Activity

1. Pair up students with different partners than yesterday, and explain that instead of staring, they are going to be listening. Listening is a communication skill that will help them in most situations. Remind them that eye contact is one way people show that they are listening. Making eye contact also helps people listen better. Today, the class will practice listening and will remember to make eye contact with their partners.

2. Instruct each pair to choose one person to speak first. That student will speak for 45 seconds about "My favorite color, food, activity, place, etc." The partner will just listen.

3. They will reverse roles as speaker and listener.

4. Now ask partners to tell each other three things they heard him or her say.

5. Wrap up the lesson by pointing out that listening is a choice we can make during a conflict. It means we do not fight, make jokes or run away. We pay attention to the other person and hear what he or she has to say. By choosing to listen closely, we can often prevent conflicts from escalating.

Work Together, Reach an Agreement

 Time Needed: 20 minutes

 Purpose: Students will work together to reach an agreement.

 Main Idea: We can resolve a conflict by working together to reach an agreement.

Materials: Oversized shorts, shirt, sweatshirt, gloves

Using This Activity

1. Introduce this lesson by saying, "Let us see if we can figure out how we can work together. I need two volunteers."

2. Tell the two volunteers that both need to wear the oversized clothes for a special event you are planning and you want them to get dressed in these clothes right away. Allow them no more than a minute to become aware of the problem that there is only one set of clothes and to try to decide what to do.

3. Take suggestions from the class about solutions to the problem. The suggestions will probably fall into three categories: They can take turns wearing the entire outfit. They can each wear part of the outfit (then they must still decide how to share it). Neither one will wear the outfit at all.

4. Ask the two volunteers to choose a solution and carry it out. How do they feel about their decision? Explain that, with the help of the class, the two volunteers reached an agreement. Bring out these ideas:

   •Agreements may involve some compromise. ("We both gave up something, and we both got something.")

   •Agreements have a time attached to them. ("We will do this for the next ten minutes. We will do it this way whenever we play.")

   •Agreements must be acceptable to all the people involved.

   •Once we accept an agreement, we are promising to follow the terms of the agreement even if we did not get everything we wanted.

Jump Ball

Time Needed: 20 minutes

Purpose: Students will identify the choice of asking a third party for help in settling a dispute.

Main Idea: Asking a third party for help is a way to handle a conflict situation.

Materials: Basketball or other rubber or foam ball

Using This Activity

1. Set up a two-on-two basketball game with the rest of the class as observers.

2. Allow the two teams to begin play. Look for any opportunity to call a disputed possession of the ball, so you can set up for a "jump shot." A player from each team will face off. You will toss the ball in the air, and each of them will try to "tip" the ball to the teammate.

3. Allow play to continue. Bring in new players, and call a jump ball again whenever possible.

4. After a short game, discuss the use of the jump ball for settling disputes about possession. Be sure students understand that the jump ball brings in an objective person to help settle the dispute. One side may be disappointed, but it is fair because it can go either way. The same is true in other conflicts. When two sides need a third party to settle an issue, one or both sides may be disappointed. Neither side may get everything it wanted.

If possible, do this activity in the gym or on the playground with larger teams. If not, clear some space in your classroom and use a foam basketball or a rubber ball, and set up a wastebasket for scoring.

Although jump balls are not used in organized basketball anymore, they are still used in informal games.

Even if a third party is not available, students can set up in advance a strategy for resolving a dispute. They can flip coins, pick numbers or draw straws.

Fables

 Time Needed: Activit 7, 15 minutes; Activity 8, 25 minutes

 Purpose: Students will identify characters' choices in fables.

Main Idea: Fables show "Choose a Response" strategies and consequences.

Materials: Aesop's fables, writing supplies

Using This Activity

Activity 7

1. Explain that fables are short stories that usually have a lesson or moral. The main characters are usually animals. Students may be familiar with some of Aesop's fables, such as "The Tortoise and the Hare," "The Lion and the Mouse," "The Fox and the Crane."

2. Read several fables in which the characters made choices in a potential conflict or dangerous situation. Ask children to identify the choices. Ask "what if" questions: What if the hare had chosen to keep running? What if the lion had chosen to swallow the mouse? What if the fox had been more sensitive to the crane's needs? What if the crane had been more hospitable?

3. Point out that all choices have consequences. We need to think about consequences before we act.

▶ Activity 8

Remind the class that fables are short stories that teach a lesson. As a class, write a fable with a "Choose a Response" idea as the moral, for example:

If you do not listen, you will not understand.

Your choices have consequences.

Sometimes you need a referee.

You cannot always have it all your way.

Try to reach an agreement.

This activity is also a lesson in working together and reaching agreement.

ACTIVITY 9

Play It Safe

 Time Needed: 15 minutes

 Purpose: Students will recognize the need to remain safe in a conflict.

Main Idea: Sometimes finding safety is the only response to choose.

Materials: None

Using This Activity

1. Emphasize that in some conflicts, safety issues may be involved (physical violence, weapons, dangerous dares). In those cases, students do not have time to consider all the choices they have learned. They must get away, get safe and get help.

2. As a group, list times when students must focus on safety first (confronted with strangers, being lost or alone, physical threats).

3. Continue the discussion by asking how children can remain safe in those situations (run away, scream, find someone to help, even struggle or kick if necessary).

4. Emphasize that these responses are very different from the ones they have been learning and are to be used in dangerous and threatening situations.

Skill Wrap-up

 Time Needed: 30 minutes

 Purpose: Students will create a display highlighting responses they have learned.

Main Idea: There are many possible responses to a conflict or putdown situation.

 Materials: Art supplies

Using This Activity

1. Review the weather discussion from Day 1. Ask if anyone has seen a rainbow. When do rainbows appear?

2. Compare a storm to a conflict. Children can break through the conflict with a rainbow of choices. Have the class work together to create a "Rainbow of Choices" wall display. On each color of the rainbow, have students write a choice available to them.

Students can also incorporate choices they learned in kindergarten and first grade:
- Tell them to stop
- Walk away
- Tell an adult

SKILL EVALUATION

Please complete this brief evaluation at the conclusion of your work on this skill.

1. Activities in this skill which worked well for me were:

2. Activities in this skill which were meaningful to my class were:

3. Activities which needed adjustments were:

4. I was unable to complete the following lessons in the two week instructional period:

5. Ways in which I can include those lessons in my plans for the remainder of the year:

6. Ways to improve this unit for future *No Putdowns* work are:

GRADE
2

SKILL 5

Build
Up

A Program for Creating a Healthy
Learning Environment by Encouraging,
Understanding and Respecting

If most of your students participated in *No Putdowns* last year, treat this lesson as review. Ask students to tell you what they remember about "Build Up." Help bring out the main point: The classroom and school are a community, and being encouraging creates a climate in the community. People can affect the emotional climate by their choices about whether or not to allow putdowns.

This last skill transfers *No Putdowns* from a school subject to practice on a daily basis. Up to this point, children have learned academically to recognize and handle putdowns. But they need practice building up themselves and others and replacing putdowns with positive statements. For many children — and adults — it is much easier to put down than build up. Review the possible reasons for putdowns — habit, modeled behavior, strong feelings. Many children do not know what to say in place of putdowns. This skill provides an opportunity to practice the important skill of building up, being encouraging and supportive.

Emphasize that Build Up does not mean giving empty compliments or simply saying the right words. The speaker has to mean them. "Build Up" is about learning to be gentle and understanding with others.

Introduction to Build Up

 Time Needed: 10 minutes

 Purpose: Students will be introduced to the skill "Build Up."

 Main Idea: Building up is the opposite of putting down.

Materials: None

Using This Activity

1. For the next ten days, students are going to get a lot of practice learning to be good to themselves and each other. But it doesn't stop after that. It is a way to think and behave always.

2. Review the previous four skills: "Think About Why," " Stay Cool," "Shield Myself," "Choose a Response."

3. Explain that "Build Up" teaches what to do instead of putting yourself or others down. Build up is the opposite of put down.

ACTIVITY 2

How to Describe Me

This activity reinforces "Shield Myself" skills and provides "Build Up" practice.

 Time Needed: 15 minutes

 Purpose: With the help of classmates, students will list three positive words about themselves.

 Main Idea: Identifying positive traits in ourselves and others is a form of encouragement.

 Materials: None

Using This Activity

1. Divide the class into pairs, and designate one student as the encourager and the other as the writer. The writer will list three positive words (or phrases) to describe himself or herself. The encourager helps the writer think of these positive attributes by telling the positive things he or she has noted about the writer.

2. Have students reverse roles and repeat the activity.

The encouragers could repeat words they have heard friends, parents or teachers use to describe the writers.

Build Up Message Board

 Time Needed: 10 minutes

 Purpose: Students will practice building up by leaving messages for classmates or the teacher.

 Main Idea: Noticing good things about other people makes it harder to put them down.

 Materials: Slips of paper, large envelope or bulletin board space

> ## Using This Activity

Today is an introduction to an ongoing activity for the class — using a class message board. Explain that there will be an envelope (or bulletin board) available in the classroom. During the remainder of this skill, students may write build-up messages to classmates or the teacher to compliment, encourage or thank them. After writing a message, students fold the slip, write the name of the recipient on the outside, and place it in the envelope or on the designated board.

Students can write notes of encouragement, appreciation or compliments:
To Jill: Thanks for helping me practice for the spelling bee.
To Rene: You played a great game of kickball today.
Mr. Rodriguez: I really like the story you read us this morning.

If your students work with computers, they might leave messages through E-mail.

ACTIVITY 4

Television Build Ups

 Time Needed: 30 minutes (or longer depending upon length of video clip)

Purpose: Students will identify build ups used in television or movies.

Main Idea: We need to be very alert to the good and bad communication habits that television and movie characters use and think about whether we want to copy them.

Materials: Video (from television show or movie) demonstrating build ups

Using This Activity

1. Introduce the video by asking students to watch for putdown and build-up situations or comments.

2. Show the video and then discuss these questions:

• What are some examples of build-up comments or behavior in the video?

• What are some examples of putdowns?

• Were there any situations that could have turned out differently if the character had used a build up (or putdown) instead? Would a different choice at that point have changed the story or outcome?

3. You may want to extend the discussion to television shows your students usually watch. Are putdowns more common than build-up situations? Why might that be?

◄ Short videos are available in your school or public library, or you might tape a television show that is popular with children.
A few video suggestions: *Pollyanna, Big Green, Charlotte's Web, Angels in the Outfield*

◄ Much of the humor on commercial television is driven by putdowns. Discuss this with students. How would they feel if those comments were directed towards them? Is it okay to use putdowns to be funny?

Grade 2 • **skill** 5

Take a Caring Walk

 Time Needed: 25 minutes

 Purpose: Students will recognize that they are part of the school community.

 Main Idea: Each person is part of the community and contributes to it.

 Materials: Chart paper and markers, or board space

Using This Activity

➤ **1.** If possible, take the class on a walk around the school building and grounds. As you walk, ask students to think about ways to improve the school physically (replace a light bulb, plant flowers, clean the playground, etc.) or emotionally (displays and exhibits, school t-shirts, etc.).

2. After the walk around the school, brainstorm ways to improve the school. Write those ideas on the board.

3. Put a checkmark next to ideas that students could actually do (for example, pick up litter in the hallways).

If walking the grounds is not possible, have students take a look around the classroom and then take a mental tour of the school.

Point out to the class that keeping the environment pleasant is a way of maintaining positive attitudes about the school. Working together to make the school a pleasant place is part of being a community.

ACTIVITY 6

Real-life Build Ups

 Time Needed: 20 minutes

 Purpose: Students will list ways they can build up others throughout the school.

Main Idea: Building up helps create a healthy community life.

Materials: Chart paper and markers, or board space

Using This Activity

1. This activity is a follow-up to the walk around the school. Ask students to think about how they can build up people throughout the school. Point out that "Build Up" skills are not only classroom skills, they are real-life skills to be used around school and home.

2. Draw a grid on the chart paper, and have students fill it in with suggestions for transferring "Build Up" skills to other school situations. ◄

Playground	Cafeteria
Bus	Hallways

The suggestions should be worded positively: "Pick up papers in the hallway," rather than "Do not Litter." "We will take turns" on the playground, rather than "Don't let anyone cut in."

3. From the chart, develop a class list of Build-Up Rules.

4. Post the rules in the classroom, or share them with other classes by posting them in the hallway outside your classroom: Build-Up Rules for _____'s Class.

Students' suggestions should be more specific than "I'll be nice to other people." For example:
Help out with jobs.
Play fair.
Listen to what the other person is saying.
Answer when someone talks to me.
Say "thank you".
Say "please".
.

Explain that cooperation is a "Build Up" skill and that by learning to work together, students are building a community where everyone can feel accepted and appreciated. You might want to talk about some of the other benefits of cooperation. For example, by working together, people can come up with more ideas for how to do something, have fun or make friends.

Grade 2 • **skill** 5

We Are There For Each Other

 Time Needed: 20 minutes

 Purpose: Students will name someone on whom they can rely and someone who can rely on them.

 Main Idea: It is important to know whom we can count on and to let others know they can count on us.

 Materials: Writing supplies

Using This Activity

1. Talk about the idea that people need each other for support, help in doing things, talking things over, providing essentials, keeping promises, love and appreciation.

2. Write this sentence on the board:

   I know I can count on _____ to

   _____.

➤ 3. Ask students to copy that sentence and fill in the first blank with a particular person (friend, relative, classmate, teacher or other adult) and the second blank with what they can count on that person to do or be for them.

➤ 4. Write this sentence on the board, and ask students to copy it and fill it in:

   _____ can count on me to

   _____.

5. Instruct students to present their " _____ can count on me" statements to the persons named the next time they see them (or during class if the statement is addressed to a classmate.)

You may want to have students fill in the sentence several more times with other people in their lives and how they count on them.

You may want to have students write several "_____ can count on me" statements to present to others. Point out that they are making a promise to the other person and they should really mean what they are promising.

Tugging Together

 Time Needed: 10 minutes

 Purpose: Students will work cooperatively to complete a task.

Main Idea: Working together can make a job easier.

 Materials: 10-20 foot piece of rope tied together at ends

Using This Activity

1. Have students sit in a circle. Place the rope within the circle, and have students hold on to it.

2. Explain that when you say, "One, two, three, go," they are all to try to stand up at the same time while pulling on the rope. If anyone falls or can't get up, have them sit down and try again. Try to continue until the class is successful.

3. Discuss the importance of working together so that all the students could pull themselves to a standing position. Can students think of other situations in which working together would be important — and fun?

◀ Watch for obvious frustration that may occur. If appropriate, process those feelings. Did students lash out or put each other down? If not, what kept them from targeting classmates?

Imaginary Gifts

 Time Needed: 20 minutes

 Purpose: Students will plan gifts for classmates.

 Main Idea: Gifts are not a duty; they are a way of saying, "I appreciate you."

 Materials: Slips of paper with names of students, box or bag, writing supplies

Using This Activity

1. Talk about the concept of "gifts." Ask students what it means to them to give a gift. Often we give gifts because we think we have to, but gifts are a way to say we appreciate and care about another person. Gifts don't have to be "things," but if they are, they don't have to be big and expensive.

2. Place students' names in a hat, and have each student draw one.

3. Ask students to complete this sentence: "If I could give a gift to_____ it would be _____ because_____.

   They are to fill it in with the name they drew from the box. The gift should be specific to that person and can be a kind act, a small item or appreciative words.

4. Have students hold onto their "gift statements" until tomorrow.

5. Discuss the old saying, "It is better to give than to receive." Ask students if they agree with that statement. Have they ever felt really excited about giving something to another person or just helping out? (A gift can be the gift of your time and help.)

It could be as simple as "If I could give a gift to Rebecca, it would be chocolate candy because she is my best friend" or "If I could give a gift to Raoul, it would be a trip to the beach because I know he likes to swim." Just being observant of the other person's likes is a build up. Tell students that you don't want them to fill in the gift with a popular toy because "it's cool." Remind them that the statement is really about the other person, not about things.

If you have planned a celebration for the final day of *No Putdowns*, students can present these gift statements to each other then.

ACTIVITY 10

No Putdowns Party

 Time Needed: 30 minutes

 Purpose: Students will celebrate the work they have done in ten weeks of *No Putdowns*.

 Main Idea: This is the completion of the formal instruction period, but the skills take a lifetime of practice.

 Materials: Depends upon activity chosen

Using This Activity

1. Have a party! The class has just completed ten weeks of *No Putdowns*. Today is a day to celebrate, have fun, feel good about themselves and the rest of the class. Partying together is also an opportunity to build community and class goodwill.

2. Ask students to name a highlight of the program, something important they learned. ◄

3. Have a grade-level or even school-wide celebration. That might mean treats in the cafeteria, a storyteller, games, a song person, etc. ◄

Remind the class that the work of *No Putdowns* is not finished. The skills will need practice and reinforcement. Continue throughout the year to make tie-ins whenever appropriate.

Students can present their "gift statements" to each other during the party.

A school-wide or grade-level celebration will take planning by teachers and even parents since parents are a part of the *No Putdowns* process. If parents are not included in the celebration, it may be appropriate to notify them that the formal instruction period of the program has ended but the work is ongoing.

Another choice is to have a "commencement" ceremony, with presentation of class certificates or other recognitions.

Please complete this brief evaluation at the conclusion of your work on this skill.

1. Activities in this skill which worked well for me were:

2. Activities in this skill which were meaningful to my class were:

3. Activities which needed adjustments were:

4. I was unable to complete the following lessons in the two week instructional period:

5. Ways in which I can include those lessons in my plans for the remainder of the year:

6. Ways to improve this unit for future *No Putdowns* work are:

NOTES

NOTES

NOTES